10 Steps to Become a Successful Mompreneur

JENNIFER COLUCCI

Published by Colucci Ventures, Inc.
www.ColucciVentures.com

1 2 3 4 5   CS   21 20 19 18 17

ISBN 978-0692892572

Cover photo and book design by Jennifer Colucci.
Back cover photo by Rebecca Cafiero, CiaoBellaFoto.com.
Copy editing by Jennifer Hillman.

DEDICATION

To my husband:
Thank you for supporting me when you believe in my ideas.
And for shutting up and getting out of my way when you don't.
It will all be worth it when you are retired; relaxing in your hammock.

To my son:
Thank you for calling me, 'Awesome Mommy' and
motivating me each day to live up to it.

CONTENTS

Introduction   7

Step 1   Discover   11

Step 2   Define   19

Step 3   Prioritize   29

Step 4   Plan   35

Step 5   Establish   65

Step 6   Build   71

Step 7   Share   93

Step 8   Organize   107

Step 9   Support   113

Step 10   Optimize   127

           Mompreneur Stories   135

           Business Ideas   155

EXERCISE CHECKLIST

☐ Billionaire Momma   12

☐ On A Mission   15

☐ Start With Why   17

☐ I Wish   20

☐ I Require   24

☐ Setting Goals   26

☐ Priorities   30

☐ Open for Business   33

☐ Little Reminders   36

☐ Products, Products & More Products   39

☐ Persona Profiles   40

☐ Brand Board   42

☐ Brand Phrases   44

☐ Monthly Profit   56

☐ Pricing Products   58

☐ Mental Board Meeting   69

☐ To-Do List   71

☐ Go-To Prospect Questions   96

☐ No Goals   100

☐ Get To Know Your Conversion Rates   102

☐ Time Blocking   109

INTRODUCTION

What is your passion?

What gets you out of bed each day, ready to take on the world? (Besides your family, of course!)

Is it the opportunity to earn an income?

Are you seeking a purpose?

When it's time to focus on you, what do you like to do?

For some women, these questions have easy answers, and this book will guide you through the process of turning ideas into reality.

For the rest of you, thinking about these questions is the perfect way to start developing yourself, your future and your level of commitment to creating your own business.

After all, building a business, no matter its size, age or industry, is like having a child.

At some point it starts as an idea; a dream. It is then methodically planned, conceived or adopted. No matter its conception, a business is created and requires constant attention. It needs to be fed resources, have quality time devoted to it and developed socially with customers. It needs to be clothed in an appropriate brand and requires caregivers and education to grow and develop into its next phase. Some businesses grow so much they leave the nest and make a life all to themselves, while some never leave the basement. When it comes to your business, it's up to you to decide the level of involvement you want to have for the duration of its life.

Do you want the comfortable, minimal responsibility of being an employee? (Similar to being a babysitter for someone else's child.)

Do you want to be part of a start-up, helping to raise a nephew business, where it's almost your own, but not quite?

Maybe you are looking to buy an existing business or join a network marketing team, where the complicated bits of starting a business have already been handled and most of the systems are in place for you to step in as an entrepreneurial parent?

Or, are you ready to have your own baby, to start your own business? Are you ready for the sleepless nights, the high-temperature scares and the soul-fulfilling adoration of being a mother and entrepreneur?

This choice cannot be made for you, nor should it be made by your circumstances. Understanding your level of commitment to your business and yourself before you begin, will set you up for success. Be honest and save yourself a lot of trouble (and a potential abandoned business baby) if you aren't ready yet. Having a baby isn't easy and neither is owning your own business. There is a lot of hard work, and the results can be so much more rewarding than employment.

Are you ready to take the first step on your mompreneur journey?

These ten steps are footprints on the path ahead of you—imprints left by other mompreneurs who have come before. They are meant to provide the advice I wish my younger self had received when I started my entrepreneurial journey, and I hope they provide a path for you to begin your own. It can feel exhilarating and terrifying to start out, and with these steps and stories, you'll see that it is possible to build a business while raising a family. You'll feel supported throughout your struggles and triumphs, and you'll know that you aren't alone. Other moms out there have looked at their dreams, decided it was time to make them a reality and are taking action. You can too! All it takes is the courage to take that first step—so let's get going!

Jenn

STEP 1: DISCOVER

Before embarking on any endeavor, it is best to discover your purpose (the reasons why you want to go on this journey), and your motivation (the things that get you through the late nights and hard times). Think of your purpose as your compass and your motivation as your fuel. Your purpose guides you toward your goal, while your motivation keeps you going, taking step after step. Your purpose needs to be so clear in your mind that distractions have no power to sway you from your path. Your motivation needs to be something so strong that nearly every obstacle will fade in comparison to the fire you feel in your soul. Your passion for the things you love to do, will be the vehicle to make everything happen.

It doesn't matter if you are selling a network marketing product, handmade items, professional service or real estate, you need to be clear on why you want to devote your time and energy doing it.

DISCOVER YOUR PURPOSE

As a mom, our children are usually the main reason we want to be a better person and have more of everything in life. Your purpose in becoming a mompreneur most likely includes a desire to provide them with more…money, time, opportunities, etc. Maybe you want to put your kids in a better school, pay down debt or cover a mortgage. These are the benefits you look to receive for the hard work you plan to invest into your business. Providing 'more' is a noble purpose that a lot of us strive for. But it's probably not your purpose in life. It makes for great motivation to keep you working hard, but your purpose is so much more! It is your purpose, such as your love of feeding people, caring for animals or capturing memories, that lights up your soul.

Exercise: Billionaire Momma

Imagine you had ten billion dollars. With every need provided for, what would be your reason for getting out of the bed each morning? (Well, okay, we know that moms have to get out of bed due to the obligations of keeping our kids on a schedule and, you know, alive!) So, imagine a kid-free Saturday morning. You've slept in an hour past your normal wakeup time and you're happily thinking of how to use your full day to yourself. With every possible option available to you, what would you want to do?

- What would you look forward to doing?
- What would make you happy?
- What do you want to accomplish in life?
- What good do you want to share with this world?

These are hard questions to ask yourself. You may even be asking the age old question, "Why am I here?" Well, what if we weren't given a specific role to play. Imagine for a moment you are here to create your own purpose, that you have within you a unique spark which never has been and never will be again. That spark can be and do so many amazing things. Why waste precious time chasing after an elusive idea of trying to find your one-and-only purpose in life? Go out there and live your right-one-for-now, purpose!

Don't wait for your billions to arrive (or a kid-free moment to occur) before you start doing what you love. Identify and follow your purpose, feed your soul and turn it into a business now. The billions will follow!

Instead of spending time worrying about the money you think you need to start living your dream, just start living it!

If you are really struggling with understanding your purpose, I recommend experiencing the "Awaken To Your Purpose" guided imagery from WayToShine.com. It was created by Lisa Busbee, a long-time client and friend of mine, as part of her program to support you to discover, love and share your unique light with the world. (You can read about my own personal experience with "Awaken To Your Purpose" in my Mompreneur Story at the end of this book.)

DISCOVER YOUR MOTIVATION

Your motivation is the fire within you that gets you up an hour early to finish a proposal—despite a sleepless night with a teething baby. It's what keeps you going when things seem to fall apart.

You need more than family to be your motivation. You love them and want the best for them and will do anything (legal and maybe even illegal) for them, but at some point (or several times) your familial motivation will get tapped out. It happens to all of us moms. We reach the end of our rope. We can feel as though the hard work we are doing for them is unappreciated. That they don't understand how hard we work. And, with kids as the only motivator, how do you handle it when things get complicated? For example, what if your business needs something at the same time as your kids? Which one do you choose? This is where resentment can grow. The effort, energy and time you invest in your business, if not appreciated by the family, can lead to you resenting them for not understanding and appreciating your efforts. Alternatively, the time you spend working, away from your kids, can lead to them resenting the business.

Your family is your 'Mom' motivation. You now need to find your Entrepreneur motivation. Together, they will create your Mompreneur motivation.

DISCOVER YOUR PASSION

Remember the giddy feeling you got when you had a crush? Your whole body felt electrified, charged up with excitement and nervousness and although you were unsure what the new day would bring, you were optimistic and hopeful for the best outcome? That's how I feel when I'm passionate about something. When I talk about my passion, I feel my entire body is flushed and practically glowing. I feel lit up and able to accomplish anything!

- What do you like to do that makes you lose track of time?
- What energizes you, no matter how long you are doing it?
- What lights you up?
- What excites you?
- What feeds your soul?

If you feel that you can't answer these questions, explore and experience new things. Try pottery, gardening, kickboxing, crafting, dancing, acting, painting, surfing, singing, writing, cooking, organizing, tinkering, modeling, speaking or volunteering. If one of these doesn't excite you, move on to the next thing to try. Stick with what you feel excited about, what pulls you in, and what makes you want to stay and experience more. During this journey of experimentation, you will be sure to find your purpose and a spark that reveals your true motivation for success.

"Passion is energy. Feel the power that comes from focusing on what excites you."

Oprah Winfrey

DISCOVER YOUR MISSION

With your purpose, motivation and passion in mind, you can create your personal mission statement.

⬚ *Exercise: On A Mission*

Start your statement with, "I am meant to…" and describe your purpose. Follow it with "… by …" and describe your passions. End it with "…because…" and describe your motivation.

It should look like this:

> "**I am meant to** be financially independent **by** sharing my network marketing products **because** I want to provide every and any opportunity for my children."

You can also change up the beginning to start with "I will…" or "I am…", based on your personal preference:

> "**I am** well-known and well-paid **by** photographing beautiful brides and their special wedding memories **because** I capture and immortalize love."

What is your personal mission statement? Write it out and place it on your bathroom mirror or make it the background of your phone or computer screen. Read it each day and believe in it!

When you know your purpose, motivation and passions you can clearly see which type of business is right for you. This way, your business won't be based on the opportunity that happens to be in front of you now, or as a result of your family situation, but purely based on your soul.

DISCOVER WHAT, HOW & WHY

While you have discovered your own personal purpose, motivation, passion and mission, your business should go through a similar exercise to clearly communicate to your customers your vision, products and philosophy.

I recommend watching the TED Talk from Simon Sinek, "Start With Why". In it, he describes the golden circle of: 'What', 'How' and 'Why'. 'What' is the product you sell, which people know well. 'How' are the details; facts of what you sell and how you created it. 'Why' is your philosophy, what you believe, your purpose and your vision for the world. Most people talk and sell from the outside in, starting with the 'What' moving into the 'How' but rarely getting to the 'Why'. However; true success stories, like Apple Inc.'s, connect and talk from the inside out, starting with their 'Why' then going into 'How'. By the time they get to the 'What' customers are already primed to purchase.

Now that all seems well and good for big Apple Inc., but what about you as a mompreneur? I'm gonna lay it on the line here—most of us aren't innovating. We aren't inventing powered flight in the 1900s, like the Wright Brothers. We aren't coding a revolutionary social networking platform in our dorm rooms like Marc Zuckerberg. Okay, maybe you ARE, but a lot of today's businesses are so similar, it is rare to be innovative and entirely new even if you do have a superior product or service.

Let's take a look at two common businesses: photography and network marketing. As a photographer, your 'What' are your pictures. You sell the same end product as traditional portraits at a department store. Your 'How', that differentiates you, are outdoor locations, natural lighting, props, and artistic editing. Yet, there are many photographers out there selling similar styles, so, how do you set yourself apart? By sharing your 'Why' and 'How' before your 'What'.

- Why do you find joy in photography?
- How do you think photography changes people's lives?

- What do you believe photography gives to people?

Thinking along these lines is even better suited toward a network marketing business. With a network marketing business, you are selling a product that many others offer as well. If you come to your business focusing on the sales or promotions perspective, (focusing on the 'What' and 'How'), you won't make the deeper connections needed to inspire raving fans and return customers. You'll be unable to generate referrals and inspire other business builders. By sharing your 'Why' you separate yourself from the masses and create a personal connection with your audience.

- Why do you resonate with the network marketing company you've chosen to represent?
- Why should your friends want to open their home to you and their friends?
- Why would someone want to be part of your team? What do you believe in?
- What lights you up?
- What do you dream about changing the world?
- Why will your network marketing company be the answer to someone else's search for their purpose?

Whether your business is that of a photographer, network marketer or something entirely different, it's important to take the time to reflect on these questions.

Exercise: Start With Why
Write down your answers to these questions and give yourself permission to think freely.

Although this time you spend may not seem productive, nor will it provide an immediate impact, it is essential work that should be done to give your business a solid foundation for success. Skipping this exercise may not hinder your business outright, but it could complicate things and slow momentum. Without this clarifying exercise, you may end up rebranding or pivoting to a different product or service down the road. Your reflection now, creates a blueprint you can use for future decision-making, which ultimately makes planning and building much easier in the long run.

STEP 2: DEFINE

It is imperative to know what you want. If you don't know where you want to end up, how can you ever get there? You must know what you want to accomplish and where you want to go. Then, make the plans to get you there.

*"Some succeed because they are destined to,
but most succeed because they are determined to."*

Henry Van Dyke

DEFINE SUCCESS

Success looks different to each individual. True, most of us see wealth as a sign of success, but as mothers, there are some days where we define success as making a home-cooked meal, (maybe even one that your kid will actually eat?) or perhaps just making it through the day without a trip to the emergency room.

The problem with the stereotypical definitions of success such as fame and fortune, extreme wealth, grand estates, expensive shoes, luxurious cars, nannies and housekeepers, is that you can get frustrated each day you haven't achieved them. We worry so much about the results of success that we often lose sight of the reasons we chose to chase after our goals in the first place.

> *"Success is believing enough in yourself*
> *to not quit on yourself."*
>
> *Megan Fischer, MegFischer.com*

DEFINE YOUR DESIRES

As moms, we spend much of our time and dreams focused on our families. The sky is the limit for what we want for our kids and our partner's careers, yet we often don't allow ourselves to want, to wish and to dream. I'm talking more than just the creation of a wish list here! I mean, anything and everything you want out of life. Do you know want you want? Have you written it down? Or, have you kept it secret in your heart, like a birthday wish, afraid to say it aloud for fear it won't come true?

Let's take a few, small steps into examining what you want out of life. Grab some paper and a pen. Writing ideas out on paper connects with you with your thoughts more than typing them on a device. It's amazing to see what flows from your mind onto paper when you allow your personal limits to be suspended for an activity like this. Plus, it is much less distracting than being exposed to everything on your phone or computer. So do it.

Seriously! Do it now!

Grab paper and your favorite writing instrument and spend a few minutes with this exercise. I promise, you'll be happy you did.

📋 *Exercise: I Wish*

Fold your paper in thirds and then again in thirds to make six boxes. Above the top row, label each column as 'Family', 'Business', and 'Self'. To the left of the first column, label each row as 'Wish', 'Want' and 'Require'.

	FAMILY	BUSINESS	SELF
WISH			
WANT			
REQUIRE			

Start filling in your wishes for your family. In this exercise, anything goes. Write three 'Wishes' down without worrying about how much money or time would be needed to make them come true. Think freely. Dig deep. Don't worry about the, "How is it going to happen?" voice inside your head. Just daydream and write down at least three of your biggest wishes.

- What do you REALLY wish will happen for your family?
- What do you wish for your business?
- What do you wish for yourself?

Do you wish that you could afford to send your kids to Harvard? Are you wishing for beach front property? Do you wish that your business would make enough money so that your husband could retire? Wish you had a wardrobe filled with high-quality items that you look and feel amazing in? Wish you weighed less, had more time to yourself or had a degree? Wish you had more self-confidence or that you could speak in front of crowds? Wish you could be different in some way, or wish you could overcome a specific fear or bad habit?

Now, move on to the next row and write three 'Wants' you have for your 'Family', 'Business' and 'Self'. This time, make them a little more realistic. Think of things you want that you could make happen if only you had just a bit more time, money or training. These are things you feel are doable with a bit of help.

Do you want a three bedroom house instead of a two bedroom for your family? Do you want your business featured in a local paper? Do you want your company to make enough to pay for a specific bill, rent or mortgage? Do you want to finish writing a book you started years ago or want to try a Zumba class? Do you want to read more, pamper yourself or dive into a hobby? Write down those wants and give yourself permission to be free in this exercise.

I know it's complicated to allow yourself to want. I experienced complicated emotions while going through my own self-exploration. I was challenged by Gerry Roberts at an event to follow his "Captain & The Crew" daily practice for 90 days. I loved his concept and excitedly jumped in, but after I pulled out my paper and got my favorite pen, I found myself unable to write. I could not put my dreams to paper. In that moment, I realized my fear and hesitation was in knowing that once I wrote them down, they existed. My wants and dreams had become real. In my head they were safe and secure. No one knew about them. They were intangible thoughts. My pen was poised above the paper, ready to write, and yet, I hesitated again. I felt ashamed that what I wanted and wished for in my head was not right, that it was too much to ask for. It wasn't right for me to want so much when I could survive on less. And then, doubt made an appearance. Even if I wrote my wishes down on paper, I didn't know if I could ever achieve them. I didn't know if I was good enough, talented enough or smart enough, for all that I wanted.

Deep down, I didn't think I deserved what I wanted.

That thought hit me hard. I was so confused by it. Here I was, a person who always worked hard in life, putting others before myself; so if I didn't deserve to be happy, then who does?

Ladies, here's the shocking truth: you deserve the chance for your dreams to come true, too! You deserve to be happy. You deserve to dream, wish and want more for your family, your business and, yes, even yourself.

I am pretty sure that despite me telling you to dream big during that last exercise, you limited yourself. So, now I want you to go back and dream bigger. Write at least one more 'Wish' and 'Want' in each box. Look over what you already wrote and try to bump it up! Get honest with yourself!

Did you wish for a three bedroom, two bath house when you really wanted a fourth bedroom to encourage more family visits? What about dreaming of an amazing kitchen and spectacular spa-like master suite? Did you write a small wish for losing weight or did you really mean to write down that you want a strong, sexy, healthy body that feels younger than ever?

Finally, in the last row, write three things you 'Require' for your 'Family', 'Business' and 'Yourself'.

Requirements refer to things like having a healthy family with a roof over your heads. For your business, maybe you require it to be in the black, ensuring it provides money instead of taking it from your family savings. For yourself, maybe it's getting more sleep!

Review the 'Wishes', 'Wants' and 'Requirements' you wrote. Can you see the differences in how you view each row?

Let's look at them in a different way. On the right of the last column, opposite 'Wishes', label it 'Thrive', opposite 'Want', label it 'Live', and opposite 'Requirements', label it 'Survive'.

Do you see how you have been limiting your thinking? By not allowing yourself to want, you have been choosing to live your life in survival mode. You may feel like you are alive when you achieve one of your wants, however; if you want to be a successful Mompreneur you must stop trying to survive and start striving to thrive!

It's time to shift your survival mindset into a thrive mindset!

☐ *Exercise: I Require*

On a new paper rewrite all of your wishes and wants, starting with the statement, "I require…"

- I require a four bedroom, three bath home with an amazing kitchen and spa-like master suite.
- I require my kids attend Harvard.
- I require a sexy, toned and strong body that feels younger than I've felt in years.

If you find yourself unable to start out with, "I require…" first write your list with "I deserve…" and then follow it up with an "I require…" list.

Now read it aloud to yourself. You aren't just requiring a roof over your head. You are requiring a very specific kind of roof. Sure, you can survive on less, but as successful mompreneurs, we expect, demand and believe that our families deserve and require more than living just to survive. You are striving to thrive!

I challenge you to continue this exercise. Review your list each day. As time goes on, you will start to see shifts in how you think and, more importantly, act in regard to your list of requirements. Just putting them on paper makes them real. Saying them aloud each day reminds yourself of what you want and gets your mind and body primed to take action so that it becomes reality.

DEFINE YOUR GOAL

Now that you've relearned how to want, let's get down to setting specific wants and goals for your business.

What amount of money would make a difference in your family's life? Is it $300 a month to cover a specific bill? How about an extra $1,000 toward rent or a mortgage? Money for kids' extracurricular activities?

What monthly amount would help you consider your business a success? At this point, you can still dream, but you should also be a realist. We would all love to earn $1,000,000per month, but if you were to create a goal for that, you'd become frustrated and give up. Instead, you need to be gentle with yourself and your business. Your business is like a child. You may just be in the planning stages, working on conceiving it, but it's not yet born into the world. Or, for some, maybe it's a toddler business of just a few years old. No matter the case, set goals appropriate to the stage your business is in. Babies need to crawl before they walk, and it's the same with your business. It's great to have intention, knowing that one day your business will grow, but you must understand that there are milestones to reach along the way.

Also, please realize that there isn't much difference between making a thousand dollars and making a million! You just need to make your first dollar and you are on your way. Repeat making that first dollar as it becomes one hundred, then on to one thousand and then on to one million and more!

The truth is, Momma, our lives bleed into our business and vice versa. I find it useful to apply business tactics like goal-setting to my personal and family life; just as I find it useful to apply toddler reward systems and teenage conflict resolution strategies to customer relationship management in business!

"Goals are dreams with deadlines."

Diana Scharf

In the corporate world, they talk about **SMART goals**. Each goal should be **Specific**, **Measurable**, **Attainable**, **Relevant** and **Time-bound**. I recommend starting with five or less goals in your life. The more you have, the less attention and action you can give to each. If you are new to goal-setting, just work on up to three. As you accomplish one, you can always set another! There is no final destination in life, the end of one journey is the beginning of another.

☐ *Exercise: Setting Goals*

Now, review the *I Require* exercise's Business Requirements and think of turning at least one of them into your first business goal. Clearly define your goal, write it down and review it. Try to improve it so that it is concise.

For example:

> The goal, "Get More Clients" is **attainable** and **relevant**.
>
> To make it a SMARTer goal, we could bind it to a **timeframe**, by writing, "Get more clients by the end of the month."
>
> Lastly, however; if we wrote, "Get two new clients with an initial order over $150, by the end of the month," that would be **specific, measurable, attainable, relevant** and **time-bound**. Now, that is one **SMART goal**!

When setting your goals, be gentle with yourself. Goals are attainable but keep in mind the time you have allocated for your business. Setting a goal to bring in $10,000 per month may sound awesome, but if you are maxed out at $6,000 per month with your availability, skipping sleep or getting extra childcare to hit that goal may create family or self-care concerns. So, please, be gentle with yourself!

A good tactic is to think of yourself as multiple resources or people in your business. Even if it's just you at your photography business, there is you the owner, photographer, editor, admin, and prop master. While you are 'You', you can't be shooting a wedding and editing yesterday's maternity photos at the same time. Understanding this is extremely helpful when you are 'the boss' and an artist (photographer, designer, baker, seamstress, etc.) and feel inspired to take on a project or client you probably shouldn't.

Imagine your business, the company entity, is the boss and you are an employee of the company. Even as CEO, the business is your boss; it tells you what it needs, when you can take vacation and when you need to step up to take the company to the next level.

STEP 3: PRIORITIZE

You can have it all—but you can't do it all at the same time. You will need to prioritize what is important to you, set boundaries within yourself, your business and your family.

Your first priority should always be yourself. As mothers, we usually give of ourselves, placing ourselves last in the queue, after our long list of family, priorities and to-dos. You can't pour from an empty cup. If you make sure to fill your well with self-love and self-care daily, it will make it much easier for you to give what is needed for your family and business.

Explore and do what feels right to you when finding your me-time. I recommend making time in the morning for yourself. Wake up a littler earlier (before the kids) and do some yoga, meditate and set your intentions for the day. If that's too complicated for you, try some time to yourself during the baby's afternoon nap or as soon as the kids are off to school. Even sipping your favorite drink, alone in your favorite spot can be enough to center yourself and connect yourself with your purpose, motivation and passions for the day ahead.

After you, comes your family. I don't recommend specifying who in the family comes first, but if you just can't see putting yourself first, then lump yourself in with everyone else in the family. You are a vital part of the family and deserve the same attention you give others.

These priorities are your operating guidelines for where you place importance in your life. At times, some tasks make take precedence over a priority if it is time-sensitive. Every so often, review your priorities to make sure you are honoring the order of importance that you set. You can also look at rearranging them for the future, or even for just a temporary span of time.

PRIORITIZE YOUR JOBS

Time for an exercise to help you prioritize everything that is important to you in your current life!

Exercise: Priorities

Grab some sticky notes or rip up a piece of paper into smaller pieces to give you flexibility to rearrange items. On each piece of paper, write out each important endeavor of your time. Include each major activity that requires your time and energy, either daily or weekly. This should include any jobs or commitments you've made to church, PTA, professional associations, sports coaching, after school activities and more. Don't forget commitments to your health, education and, of course, your new business baby.

The more priorities on your list, the more complicated it can be to order their importance. When I first started this exercise, I had a list of 12 priorities! It was no wonder I grew overwhelmed in trying to achieve everything I wanted, as well as trying to manage my time between them. The simpler your priority list, the better. I now only have five; I'm much happier and set up for success instead of feeling constantly overwhelmed.

Look over your priorities and see how you can consolidate or group things together. Now start prioritizing! Pick up each piece of paper and shuffle them around until they are listed in the order you want. The most important item needs to be first with the least important last.

After your priorities are ordered by importance, write them out on a new sticky note and place them on your bathroom mirror, fridge, desk or dashboard of your car.

Are you artistic or crafty? Turn it into artwork and frame it for your desk or save it as the background on your phone. If you keep a journal or diary, write your priorities on the inside cover where you can see it each time it's opened.

PRIORITIZE YOUR TIME

Next, think about each priority and decide how many hours a week you dedicate to each. There are only 24 hours in a day — at least six-to-eight which should be used for sleep, which leaves 16-18 hours in a day for everything else. Remember, standard jobs usually require four-to-eight hours per day.

How much time can you dedicate to your business baby? What is your ideal mompreneur work week? Are you happy to work a full 30-40 hours a week? Do you prefer part-time hours of 10-20 hours during the week? Do you only want to work weekends?

Break up your days and weeks into hourly chunks and get real with yourself. Do you actually have the time available that your business needs to make it as successful as you want? No matter your industry, if you treat your business like a hobby it will pay like a hobby; if you treat it like a business it will eventually pay like a business. That doesn't mean working part time on your business won't make it a success— it's about the effort you DO with those few hours that defines your success. If you just go through the motions, but don't actually produce income, product or results, then you are playing at the business and not working it.

Step 3: Prioritize

"Part-time is better than no-time."

Shankari Paradee, SewlSister.com

I've fallen into the trap of just going through the motions myself. Working from home and working for ourselves has its own unique challenges. It is easier to get distracted. Manpower and time may be limited based on your other duties around the house. And, for some, if you are the only one in the business, it can also get lonely. Social networking platforms may seem to be the easy way to connect with customers, but beware, you can quickly lose productive hours scrolling through others' lives instead of creating your own. A trick I use to manage this distraction is to not use social networks on my work device. For those using laptops for business, like photographers or web designers, don't allow your favorite social networking sites to be open. Make a conscious effort to only use your phone or tablet for responding to customers or allot dedicated time in your schedule for social marketing.

PRIORITIZE YOUR CALENDAR

We all have our normal routines—the order and process in which we get ready in the morning. Routines are habits we do so often we don't even think about them. For your business you don't want to find yourself mindlessly following a routine, but you do need a schedule. A child's routine (whether regimented or loose) provides an understandable pattern to their days and gives their mom some sort of order to the chaos! A business needs a schedule for the same reasons: structure and organization.

As a mompreneur, you will not survive, let alone thrive, without a schedule. Winging it is for hobbyists. If you are serious about your business, you need to be serious about your schedule. When you own your own business, you aren't the boss of you—your schedule is the boss.

☐ *Exercise: Open For Business*

Now that you have ordered your priorities, you can create your schedule. Start by setting aside a few hours, (kid-free if possible), to set up your first calendar. You will need your family, personal and business calendars to ensure everything gets the attention it requires. For this exercise, I recommend printing a weekly calendar that includes hourly marks.

Look at an average week or month and block out the activities you have already committed to, like church, PTA, sports, etc.. Block out the time you spend at your day job, taking care of kids (dropping off at school, sports, music classes, etc.) as well as cooking and cleaning time too.

Next, look at your blocked out calendar to see where there are gaps. How many hours a day, week and month do you have available to dedicate to your business? What specific days and times can you commit to your business's working hours? Essentially, when are you 'open for business'? Reserve that time in your calendar so that you are less likely to schedule anything else during your dedicated business time.

STEP 4: PLAN

With a clear understanding of your priorities and a rough idea of your hourly investment in your business, you can now start planning!

PLAN FOR YOUR SANITY

Us moms don't have the luxury of much personal, quiet time. Stay-cations or getaways to work on your business are probably not options for you. You'll need to work hard to find or make time for your new business baby. And, just like when you came home with a newborn, you'll probably find yourself up in the middle of the night working on building your dreams. You may even think, "Why did I ever do this? It's too hard." And suddenly, your business baby will coo and smile at you and make it all worthwhile.

Keep in mind, building a business is a journey. The first steps may be easy as you are excited and motivated, then things may get tedious and boring. You will get stretched beyond your comfort zone and feel fear and hesitation to move forward. In those moments, remember you are growing and learning, preparing for the next step in the journey that is your business and success.

So, how do you keep sane while dreaming up your business and taking care of the kiddos? Leave yourself little reminders throughout the day to keep your purpose and goals on your mind.

[ ] *Exercise: Little Reminders*

Place reminders around the house. Write up some inspirational quotes, and place them strategically around your house so that they are little reminders for you to view throughout the day.

Wake up a little bit earlier to have quiet time and an herbal tea while reviewing your personal and business missions.

Write daily or weekly intentions of tasks or goals you'll take action upon. Place them on your nightstand, bathroom mirror, car dashboard, fridge, or computer (anywhere and everywhere) to remind you of your commitment to the business.

Carry a touchstone, that signifies your commitment, determination and excitement to make forward progress, no matter how small the step, every day. A touchstone could be a piece of jewelry like a bracelet or ring, special keychain, or even phone case or background image. Each time you touch them, or they catch your eye, (or are grabbed by your toddler), you'll be reminded of your goals and the actions you have committed to take.

These ideas are meant to keep your business at the forefront of your mind. They are not to be a reminder of all the things you 'should' be doing. You will accomplish what you can when you can. It's not worth the self-guilt to allow negative voices in your head getting too loud. No matter your day job, be it the CEO of a billion dollar company or a hobby crafter, your most important job in life is as a mother. You have the amazing honor to shape the life of another person, someone who unconditionally loves you even when they say they don't! It's your job to nurture, protect, teach and mold your children into the best human being they can become. As you know, it's an awesome responsibility with a lot of rewards and challenges!

So, please: don't EVER feel bad for spending the day with them at a theme park, beach or an exploration of the backyard. Your business (and the dishes) can wait. Your little one will only be little for so long.

That being said, there are still ways you can find pockets of time to spend with your kids and work on your business.

Find a notebook that fits in your purse and carry it everywhere! Are your kids playing at the park? Instead of scrolling through a social network, pull out your notebook and jot down ideas. Make task lists, write an article or sketch out ideas for a new product. Pull out your notebook at sports practices, in lines at theme parks, at the beach and even at fast food restaurants with play structures! Pull out your notebook anywhere you feel confident that your kids are safe and you aren't needed to be fully present. Be sure to keep extras of your favorite pens or pencils with you too (you don't want to be stuck using leftover crayons from lunch at your child's favorite restaurant)!

I wrote this book in two notebooks while traveling to several different beaches, parks, doctor offices and my family's favorite splash pad. I never left home without it. The thing is, you never know when you'll be inspired and need to jot an idea down. I've come up with ideas in a pickle aisle at the grocery store and even spent a few bath times sitting on the floor writing while my son played in the tub.

PLAN FOR INSPIRED IDEAS

As I mentioned before, random flashes of ideas can come to us at any moment. When they are full-fledged concepts that are not in your usual train of thought, I call them inspired ideas. They are gifts from your subconscious or higher power. Most people experience a thought and don't think anything of it. Some people receive an idea, play around with it in their head for a bit, imagine what could happen with it and release it back where it came from. Those who take note of an inspired idea write it down and claim it as theirs, while fewer still act on it, creating and birthing it into the real world.

You have the power to choose how you want to handle your inspired ideas.

Keep in mind, nothing happens without thought and motivation. If you have those two things, an idea and a motive, everything else can be figured out!

My best inspired ideas come to me when I am doing something routine: washing dishes, putting away laundry, exercising or walking. Thanks to being stuck in California freeway traffic, I often do my best creative thinking while driving.

If you spend a lot of time in the car too, the first step toward creative thinking on the road, is releasing the stress and frustration of feeling 'stuck' in traffic. Instead, view it as an opportunity for thinking, planning and dreaming. If the kids are with you, this could be a great time for relaxed thinking, especially given the fact that they are strapped in the back, where there isn't much trouble they can get into. Think freely and daydream! When you get to your destination, quickly jot down your ideas into your notebook, or leave yourself a voice memo on your phone.

Also, when searching for inspiration, listen to classical or other instrumental music. This type of music stimulates your mind, yet won't be able to distract you with lyrics. (Plus, it's a great way to convince your little guy to share the music with you and give the sing-a-long playlist a break!)

PLAN YOUR BUSINESS

How are you going to make money? All your motives, purpose and dreams aren't worth anything if you don't know how your business will make money. Even non-profit foundations need to know where their money will come from.

At this point, don't worry about detailed particulars like packaging and pricing. First, consider your business model. Are you selling a tangible product such as handmade quilts or clothing? Digital products like music, online courses or content memberships? Providing a service such as web design, photography or gardening? Each type of business model has its own set of opportunities and challenges. Knowing your business model will also assist you when researching marketing ideas and clearly defining your business to others.

☐ *Exercise: Products, Products and More Products*

So, what will your business provide to others? Why will your customers give you their money? Set a timer for five minutes and write down every single idea you can think of regarding products, services or other revenue-generating item that may be available from your business.

Don't allow doubts to creep into your mind during this free writing time. You don't need to worry about the feasibility of executing these ideas right now, or whether or not you know how to make them happen. This is a brain dump of all the ideas that you have bouncing around in your head. Dream big and have fun with this exercise. Don't stop writing and thinking until the five minutes are up and you have at least 10 items on your list.

Your initial ideas may be straight forward: cupcakes, photography sessions, quilts, etc. but think beyond the initial product. As a baker, you can also offer custom cookie designs and cookie-decorating classes, (maybe even geared toward kids, Moms' Night Outs or bachelorette parties). Photographers could offer upgrades like fashion styling or props for sessions and even training walks with tips for capturing local landmarks. Quilters could upsell products with personalized embroidery or sell patterns of quilt designs online.

Keep this list bookmarked in your notebook, as you will get ideas throughout your day. Once you start thinking ideas about all of your opportunities, you'll experience welcome flashes of insight, random "Hmm, that might work" ideas and more. While you may not see these ideas as viable now or you don't know how to make them happen, writing them down for the future frees up your mind from remembering it along with everything else you have going on as a mother and business owner.

PLAN FOR YOUR CUSTOMERS

Before you start going too far into the details of your products and business you need to understand your customers.

- Who are they?
- What do they believe?
- What do they worry about?
- What do they dream about?

You can start off with basic demographic information, but it's more effective to connect with your customers' wants and worries, so that you can discover who they really are.

📖 *Exercise: Persona Profiles*

Think of the different types of prospects or customers your business will have. You may just have one, or, you may have several different personas. Each persona will have a different way of looking at your product. For a photographer, your persona may be of an expectant mom with a love for all things modern; for a network marketer, you'd have at least two personas: a product consumer and a business builder. For a blogger, you'd most likely have a persona for your audience and a persona of your advertisers. Or, you may have a persona for each product category or offering.

Next, start to create a detailed profile for each different persona you listed. Write out responses to the questions below as if they were the ones answering the questions themselves.

- Are they male or female?
- Where do they work or go to school?
- How much money do they earn?
- What are their interests? What kinds of movies, music, books, or food would they like?
- Who do they look up to? Who are their role models?

- Where do they live? How do they live?
- How do they get around?
- How do they spend their money? Where do they shop?
- What do they worry about?
- What excites them?
- What are they trying to improve in their life?

Give your persona a name to make them even more real to you! And, of course a profile isn't complete without a photo, so go online to find a royalty-free portrait that matches your persona. Or, if you based your profile on a real customer, see if you can use one of their photos. This photo shouldn't be published and should be used to help you connect with your customers when you are working on your brand or writing copy.

Why is knowing your customer important? You need to know them in order to create a product they not only need, but love. As an artist, it is intuitively easier to create something for 'Mary', a career woman with a love for gold, heels and hashtags, than to create something for an unknown user of my product. Even if you aren't an artist in the traditional sense, every act of creation is an art form. My accountant handles my taxes as deftly and with as much precision as a painter with a brush. So, as entrepreneurial artists, our art will resonate and connect more authentically when we create it for someone specific, even if that someone is imaginary and only lives in our head. Your work will resonate with those who believe, worry and dream, in the ways that your persona profile does.

Have you ever watched kids playing with a bubble machine? Some kids stand in front of the blower gleefully startling themselves as the bubbles pop all over them. Others eye a specific bubble and chase it across the field, oblivious to all the other bubbles floating around them. Playing at the park one day with my son, I saw this scene play out. He stood at the machine while I watched as a little girl toddled off the playground, to chase one bubble. With the breeze, it was highly unlikely she would be able to catch this bubble, but she kept at it. At first, I admired her tenacity to stay true to her purpose, despite all the other bubbles surrounding her. But, I realized something: she was expelling a lot of energy in chasing after that one bubble that was always just beyond her grasp. Meanwhile, my son stood close to the bubble source, full of joy and glee as any and all bubbles burst upon him.

Think about how you go about getting customers. Are you investing so much on one prospect that you ignore all of the other bubbles around you? Or, even worse, does that one special customer you have, take you too far away from your other prospects?

Documenting your ideal customer through persona profiles is the first step to avoiding these situations. The second step is knowing where to find them. Throughout the process, be aware of the time and energy you spend on the chase.

Recognize anyone in your persona profiles? Many times we create a product that we would want to buy, so as you write a profile you may recognize a lot of your own wants and worries. That's okay! (If not, that's okay too!) As you go through the process of building your business, remember this: your purpose is your compass. Your customer personas are the different paths to your business' success. If you leave the path you set out for, the journey will get bumpy and more complicated to travel. At those times, choose to get back on your persona's path, or create a new path with a new or edited persona.

PLAN YOUR BRAND

Imagining the look, feel and vibe of your business may be easy, but communicating it clearly to your graphic designer, printer, manufacturer and most important, your customers, can get complicated.

[ ] *Exercise: Brand Board*
When designing brands for my clients, I recommend using a digital board, like Pinterest, to collect images and photos that convey the look, feel,

emotions tone and soul of the brand. (You can also manually create a board by using a poster board, glue and magazine cutouts, however; a digital board is easier to share.)

If you have trouble finding inspiration for your brand's mood board, try visualizing the brand by imagining it as a person. What does she wear? How does his voice sound? What do they smell like? What music do they listen to? What are their favorite hobbies? What is their favorite drink? How do they make you feel after interacting with them? Add images to your mood board that convey who your brand would be as a person.

After you have several pins on your board, review it and remove anything that doesn't fit well with the rest. Or, if you feel really drawn to a specific image, search for similar inspiration to add to your brand board.

Your brand board is also a great way to communicate colors. Collecting images in the colors you envision allows you to clearly define the color palette you want to represent your company. This is of great help to your designers and will save you (and them) time and money. Keep in mind though, you need to remember your customers' personas, and what they will want from your brand. Your preferences aren't helpful unless they reflect the desires of your customers. What matters most is what your customers like, what colors and fonts resonate with them and what they think of your product.

If you have someone working with you to help create your brand, you can invite them to add pins to your digital board, too. If you're using Pinterest, they allow you to have private boards so that others can't see what you are working on unless you invite them to join you.

PLAN FOR YOUR VOICE

Now that you've discovered your audience, it's time to find the voice of your business. Your voice is the tone, manner of speech, phrases and general language you use when communicating from your business. It should resonate with your customers and your product. Every email, social media post, web page, product description, blog post, video, webinar, eBook, tutorial, and receipt will all be written in this voice which speaks to your ideal customer.

Professional service providers, like accountants or therapists, will most likely have a more traditional and respectful tone. Handmade boutiques may use country charm and colloquialisms. Success coaches who pride themselves on pushing their clients beyond their comfort zones may take an in-your-face, irreverent tone and may even use profanity.

Exercise: Brand Phrases

To discover your business voice, make a list of words you relate to and like using, as well as a list of words you don't like. For instance, a coach may relate to the words, coach, mentor or guide, but shy away from guru or maven—likewise, another may love guru and dislike the term coach. There aren't any right or wrong answers here. You are designing and creating YOUR business. Getting clarity with these lists will help you further down the road when you write (or hire someone to write) your copy. Word lists like these help ghost writers, marketing specialists and virtual assistants better understand your brand, your voice and how to communicate on your behalf.

I recommend doing this exercise before picking out domain names and filing official business documents. I've encountered several instances of business and domain name changes after they have already launched, because they realize (some sooner, some later) the name doesn't resonate with their customers or themselves. In one instance, a client felt lackluster about their business for nearly a year and through this exercise we uncovered her dislike of being in the spotlight which was contradictory to her business and domain name. She didn't believe in the name and her lack of belief was passed on when she talked to prospects, causing them to be unsure of her and her business as well. It took us three different logo and web site redesign efforts before realizing the real problem was the name. It contained two terms the client really didn't feel connected with.

So, if you're already further along, don't feel discouraged; if you start to see disconnects in areas, you can always make improvements (rebrand, tweak, optimize, etc.), it's just much easier to start off on the right foot when you can.

PLAN YOUR IDENTITY

While your company name takes precedence, thinking through your domain name, taglines, social networking accounts, hashtags and even telephone numbers, all together, will allow your business to have a consistent identity.

Your business name should convey either who you are, the benefit your products or services provide and maybe even your location. You can make up a word that is entirely new, like Google or Uber, but keep in mind it will be harder and more expensive to gain brand awareness. (Although, mystery often breeds curiosity.)

Don't decide on a business name until you've researched to see if the domain name is available! It is just plain awful when you figure out the perfect name, only to have to add dashes in your domain name or get an unusual extension (like .net, .guru, .group, etc.). At best, it can confuse people trying to get to your site and, at worst, it can send people to the wrong site, potentially a competitor.

Domain Name

Spend quality time thinking of your domain name. As a service provider like a photographer, therapist or artist, you may want to use your name. However, search engines like relevant search engine keywords in your domain name. For example, JenniferColucciPhotography.com will usually rank higher than JenniferColucci.com when people search for photography.

When brainstorming domains, check out Pana Bee. It's a great tool that allows you to see alternative spellings and word combinations and it will tell you if a domain name is available or not. This will save you a huge amount of time as you won't have to check them individually.

If you find the perfect domain but it says it's already registered, you still may have a chance to get it. People will register domains and **park** them, meaning they aren't using them on a web site; they're just saving them to use later on, or to sell. If a domain is registered already, try visiting it in your browser. If a working web site displays then it's highly unlikely you can get that domain. If you get an error page or a service provider page, like GoDaddy or NetSol, then you still have a chance! On these pages there will usually be a link to show your interest in purchasing the domain from the owner. Some domains aren't too expensive while other premium domains can be over $1,000. From my point of view, it never hurts to ask! You never know what could happen. Another option is to see when the domain expires as it may be available to purchase in a few months. Some providers, like Go Daddy have a backorder option which lets you reserve the right to purchase the domain after it expires, or bid on it if there are multiple interested parties.

Social Media

Also check relevant social networking sites like Facebook, Twitter and Instagram, to be sure that they have accounts available with your name. Try to be as consistent as possible, especially with Twitter and Instagram.

For social media purposes, it's also recommended to research any hashtags you may want to use. Although hashtags like #successfulmompreneur or #mompreneurlife aren't reserved for one purpose or company, it is important to review the ones you plan on using to see what type of posts are already associated with it.

Logo

Your logo will most likely consist of text in a specific font, color or spacing and may include an additional mark or graphic. If you are drawn to a specific motif like butterflies and want it incorporated within your logo, you'll want to find a way to reflect that idea in your company name. Think of metaphors for inspiration or even research foreign language translations, like 'mariposa'. During this phase, you can create a logo yourself, purchase one that is predesigned, hire a designer to work with you one-on-one or reach out to a crowd-sourcing service like LogoTournament.com to host a design contest. Whichever option you choose, make sure you own the rights or have the correct licenses for how you intend to use it. This is especially important if you are buying artwork from a royalty-free library like iStockPhoto, Creative Market or even Etsy. Certain licenses restrict being able to sell anything using the artwork or may have run limits on how many website page views or printed pieces you can make for each license you hold.

PLAN YOUR COMPANY DESCRIPTIONS

Remember, YOU are the momma of this new business baby. It's up to you to tell others about how adorable and awesome it is! To do this, you will need a few different statements to describe your company. You'll need a standard one for your business's Facebook page or LinkedIn company page, a longer one for your Etsy shop page and something very short for Instagram and Twitter. You'll also need a few paragraphs for your web site's 'About' page.

During this writing phase, don't worry about being perfect—just get words out on paper. It doesn't matter if you start with gibberish. You STARTED! After that, you can edit and refine the words until you get them the way you like; or, send what you have to a copywriter to finish for you.

"You can always edit a bad page.
You can't edit a blank page. "

Jodi Picoult

If you have trouble writing or think writing isn't your thing, use a word processing software like Microsoft Word, which offers a speech-to-text mode, or you can use the speech-to-text function on your phone to write an email to yourself. One of my clients speaks so eloquently and passionately about her products and yet when she writes content it lacks her personality. When we worked on writing her content together, she thought it was my prose making all the difference, but the truth is, I was just transcribing the words flowing out of her mouth. Some people get tongue-tied when they have a pen in hand or stare at a blank computer screen. The tools of writing can actually impede the act of capturing what you have to say. A tool like speech-to-text, or even recording a video of yourself, removes that block and allows the words to flow. If it's awkward to see the text typing as you talk, tap up a photo of a friend on your computer monitor or better yet, find a photo that represents your ideal customer, and imagine you are speaking to them instead.

Many of my clients stumble through the content writing process of building their websites. Some can describe their products and services easily, but when it comes to their 'About' page, they get stuck. My favorite way to help them come up with language is to have them write an email to a lost contact and share their new endeavor. I have them start with a specific person so that they don't get confused with trying to communicate with a mass audience. By pretending to communicate with just one person, you end up writing on a deeper level to your customers. Try it! Start with, "Dear Jane…"

Your Tagline

A tagline is a phrase or sentence, using three to seven words, that embodies your brand and conveys its essence. Nike's "Just Do It" and Skittles' "Taste

The Rainbow" are examples of taglines that both start with verbs instilling a sense of urgency and command. Arbonne's "Pure, Safe, Beneficial" and Wrangler's "Real, Comfortable, Jeans" taglines speak to the quality of their product and philosophy. Etsy's "Your place to buy and sell all things handmade" and Pinterest's "The World's Catalog of Ideas" are more descriptive and tell you exactly who they are.

A tagline is a great marketing tool but that doesn't mean you have to include it in your logo. When you design your logo, know that you can have multiple variations. They should all have a similar look, but depending on whether they're used for a web site header or a social media profile image, you may want them with and without taglines included.

After you have created a tagline you like, you should do a registered trademark search to ensure the phrase isn't protected by another entity.

Your Company Short Description

A company's short description is made of two-to-three sentences that are used on social media pages as a quick bio about the company or brand. They should be straight-forward and enticing. Due to the short length, brevity is key. You don't want to write your business's entire life story here (nor your own). Your goal is to give readers enough info, with relevant keywords for search engines, so that you can get them interested to click for more on your site or feed.

Your Company Long Description

Next up, is your main company bio or 'About' copy. At three-to-five paragraphs, here is where you can go into detail about your history, philosophy, product line and founders. Your intention shouldn't be to simply share facts. This is where you connect with your audience and customers. You may feel like starting at the beginning, about who you are, when you started the company, etc., but I prefer to start with a story about the product or a satisfied customer. You can also pose a question to connect your experience with readers like. "Have you ever wished…"

It's good to think of this like a first date. You've had the brief coffee date (usually on your social media) and now this is the sit-down dinner. You should share the basics, but keep it interesting so that they are excited for the next 'date', which could be opting into your email list, reading your blog or making a purchase!

Your Elevator Speech

You'll also need to write and practice your elevator speech. This is usually made of one-to-two sentences which you can recite in 10-15 seconds, in response to that age old date question, "So, what do you do?"

Our natural response to this question usually starts out with, "I am…"

- I am a stay-at-home mom.
- I am an infant sleep consultant.
- I am a photographer.

Notice how we label ourselves with a quick response? But, when you think of it, the question doesn't ask who ARE you? Instead, answer the question they actually asked, which is "What do you DO?"

Instead of responding with, "I am…" start with an action verb like "I help" or "I give." Describe the benefits your products or services provide to your customers. Again, the point is to entice your audience to want to know more and ASK for more info! Don't just prepare the initial responses; practice responding to their follow-up questions too. For example, how will you answer the questions below?

"Wow, how do you do that?"

"How did you get into that?"

"How did you come up with that?"

Here are some sample conversations to help you:

Person: "What do you do?"

Your Response: "I help moms get a full night's sleep."

Person: "Oh, I need that! How do you do that!"

Your Response: "I provide in-home sleep training for newborns and toddlers."

Or...

Person: "What do you do?"

Your Response: "I capture memories and let families cherish them forever."

Person: "That sounds sweet, how do you do that?"

Your Response: "I visit people's homes and photograph everyday life of their children."

Your Title

One of the biggest hurdles I've seen my clients encounter is in coming up with their personal business title. It may seem straight forward for a photographer or graphic designer; however, just like your elevator speech, having a unique title can spark conversation and make a deeper connection.

For example, for a dog walking business, you could use a descriptive title like Dog Walker or something playful like Canine Liberator. (You can also omit a title if your business name and logo clearly define your product and services.) If you do choose a creative title, make sure it fits your brand, voice and resonates with your target audience. The Canine Liberator title might work great for a stark, red or black, grunge, revolutionary vibe, but not so much so for a zen, green, calming doggie day spa.

In the corporate world, titles have specific meaning. They don't always reflect what you do in the company as much as they show where you are on the corporate ladder. A corporate card says a lot about you and your importance within that organization. In the entrepreneurial world, however; your business card, like all of your marketing materials, isn't about you—it's about your customers and how you can solve their problems and better their life.

During networking events, I'll see cards that boast titles of CEO, President and Founder. All this really tells me, is that the individual started their own business. It doesn't tell me what they do or how they can help me.

Don't get me wrong, it's awesome to act in those roles for business and I even hold those position in my own corporation, but I don't use those titles on my business cards or social media profiles. They just are not useful as a means for attracting business or for use in filling out your work history. I recommend that even if you wear all of those hats (and probably a few more) use a title that empowers you to close deals and take your career to the next level. For example, if you're a graphic designer, photographer or handmade designer, try using the title of Creative Director. It implies a position of authority, decision-making skills and the vision to direct, while keeping your hands involved with the day-to-day creating.

Are you still unsure about what to call yourself? Research people on LinkedIn and other job sites who have similar positions in companies within your industry and see which titles they use. Research can spark new ideas, yet always be true to yourself and your brand—what works for one doesn't mean it will work for you. Think of it like the process of discovering your parenting style. You may have seen someone on TV or at the park do something and told yourself you would NEVER do that as a parent. Or maybe you follow someone on social media and think, "I'd like to try that with my child." While you are inspired to act based on that interaction, you don't drop everything and become that person. Branding, titles, descriptions and writing are like that. Take the time to find inspiration, uncover your true brand and make tweaks as you go. Do not simply do the same as someone else just because it worked for them (or another successful millionaire in your industry). You aren't them and your business isn't theirs, even if it is the same type of business. There is a reason why there are thousands of successful photographers—each one has a different style, eye for a shot, equipment and editing preferences. For network marketers, it is the representative's story, personality and audience that makes each business different. You will find more contentment in the journey and eventual success by being true to yourself and your own brand than by constantly emulating others.

It's important to continue to inspect and learn from others (especially their success stories) but don't ditch all you have done to become 'them'. Understand what you offer and focus on being YOU! Big changes to who your company is and what it stands for is confusing to customers, creating uncertainty, reducing their trust and purchases.

Small tweaks and trying new product lines, promotions, and market research don't change your brand but can help it grow. Emulating other brands can seem like pivoting, potentially alienating your existing customers and putting you back at square one to find new customers. Even worse, it can make your brand feel like a knockoff of the company you are mimicking and won't showcase the true original you are to your prospects!

PLAN YOUR STYLE GUIDE

After you have planned your brand, logo, colors, fonts and photography style, document them all together in a style guide. Provide details about font families, sizes and styles used during different situations on your website, like headlines vs. body copy and more. Display your brands in an image file and list their RGB, Hex and Pantone codes as well, so that it makes it easy for you to copy and paste. Include any slogans, phrases, words and hashtags that you use regularly when writing or speaking for the business. Also include your mood boards, logo, existing marketing materials or photography that reflect your brand. If you have additional information, links to your social networking profiles or contact information, be sure to add them as well. Your style guide should be kept up to date with any tweak you make as your business transforms and grows. It should be shared with designers, photographers, virtual assistants, writers or marketers to get them up to speed on your brand and identity while ensuring their work is in line with your ideals too.

PLAN FOR COMPETITION

Knowing information about your competitors and industry empowers you to make educated decisions on things like products, prices and marketing. It can also save you from enduring costly mistakes as you learn what works (or doesn't work) from a competitor.

Find at least five competitors to your business. One should be a big, 'pie-in-the-sky' competitor who represents what you want your company to become. At least three should be local, direct competitors, maybe slightly bigger, but as similar to your business as possible. This will give you a feeling for what your business should be doing now, as well as growth ideas for its future. For now, do competitive research to see what your competitor's brands stand for, learn about their perfect customer, where they advertise, study their image and experience how they make a customer feel.

It's a good idea to do research on other brands that are complementary to your brand and ideal customer. They may be in a different industry, but have the same ideals and attract similar customers. These companies may offer an opportunity to collaborate and create successful promotions together. A great example is a wedding photographer and a stylist. You both have the same perfect customer (a bride on a budget), so you can both offer services jointly as a package or provide each other as referral business. This is a great alliance—you aren't competitors, your products or services complement each other and you share the same customer base. If you identify a complementary business that you'd like to work with, invite the business owner or a manager out for a coffee or lunch so that you can learn about their business, history and collaborative opportunities. Reaching out to talk to an existing business that caters to your ideal customers or has similar branding to you, allows you learn from others, saving yourself time and money along the way.

The intent of competitive research is to have an understanding of the marketplace you plan to join. This information can impact the way you price your products, the types of products you offer and how you communicate. It's not meant to make you feel discouraged about your business. There will always be people or businesses further along the path than you are, so don't let that stop you from enjoying or even starting your own journey.

We all have insecurities. I endured a lot of negative self-talk about partnering with my friend in her personal development company. Deep down, I knew I wanted to be her partner, but I'd see the people I looked up to in our industry and felt inadequate. I had so much I wanted to share with others, yet couldn't stop thinking, "Why would anyone want to learn from me, when they could learn from others who are better than me?" Others out there had more experience, products and connections, but I have Lori Harder to thank for shutting down that negative voice in my head. I was attending one of her motivational events, the Bliss Project, and she was answering a question from the audience. I don't remember the question, just her response of "Look, we all have the same message."

That answer totally resonated with me. Here was one of those people who was further down the path than me who has a similar mission to positively impact women's lives, just like I dream of doing. And, in that one moment, it hit me. She is right. We do all have the same message. We are all selling something that someone already has. We all have moments of doubt, thinking, "Why bother when someone else already has?"

That's when I realized we aren't really selling a message, product or service. We are selling ourselves, and THAT is our unique factor. I realized that people will want what I have to offer, because I have a unique blend of purpose, motivation, passion, experience and personal story. And, so do you!

The world has never seen someone exactly like you before. YOU have a unique blend of purpose, motive, experience and personal story the likes of which this world has never seen before. And, the world will never again see this version of you again. The most important asset in your business is YOU. It's not your product, brand, or your pricing structure—it's YOU! When you believe you've got what it takes and share that confidence with your customers and employees, great things can be accomplished. If you don't think you can do it, that there is someone better out there, then your customers and employees will sense it too—and may choose to leave you for that 'better' someone elsewhere.

PLAN YOUR PAY

Yes, it's time for some number crunching. This is the fun part of figuring out how much you want to be paid for the hard work of caring for your business baby. (Please remember to consult with a tax attorney. I'm summarizing how I think about things for my own business purposes; I am not stating that I am an expert in this area and my advice does not replace that of a certified tax consultant!)

In most cases, as the owner of a start-up business, you usually don't pay yourself a salary. Your income comes directly from the profits of the company. Being that you won't be getting a salary, you want to ensure that your required income can be derived from the business's profits.

Exercise: Monthly Profit

First, decide your monthly profit requirements. You can pick a random number, base it off of your family's budget requirements or your previous position's salary. If you are coming from a salaried position, take your salary and divide it by 12 to get your monthly income requirement.

Whichever choice you make, when you are self-employed an extra tax is due to cover social security. You'll also want to consider that health insurance costs for self-employed individuals are higher than those employed. So, take your monthly target and multiply it by at least 1.4 (this is your monthly goal plus an extra 40%), to get a more accurate rate that reflects a similar salary.

PLAN YOUR PRODUCT PRICING

After you've done some competitive and complementary research, you should have a general idea of market prices for your ideal customer and product packages or tiers. You can either choose to follow market trends or divert from them by offering lower or higher pricing. Again, it all depends on your brand. If you are creating a luxury brand and providing high value, your pricing should reflect that. If your brand is about affordability or DIY then a lower price may be prudent. Either way, keep in mind that a listed price is the highest price you'll ever get. If you want to run promotions, consider what those might be and reverse engineer your prices from your discounts and costs.

If you want to be a business owner, you've got to know your numbers and some basic business math. You should never price anything without knowing how much it costs you to make it, sell it and earn a profit. Without knowing, you run a high risk of not making a profit and feeling frustrated at working hard for much less than you anticipated.

Visit SuccessfulMompreneur.com to get spreadsheets to help you along with these exercises.

Product Cost of Goods

Let's plan a product's pricing. Pick one of your main products to go through this exercise. I'll be using a physical product from an online retailer: a teddy bear.

☐ *Exercise: Pricing Products*

First, list all the materials that will be used to create the finished product. List the amount you need and the pricing for that amount. Add up each item to get the product's **Total Material Cost**.

MATERIAL	REQUIRED	PRICE	COST
Fabric	.25 yards	$8/yard	$2.00
Stuffing	8 oz.	$12.99/32 oz. bag	$3.25
Safety Eyes	2	$2.49/4 pack	$1.25
		Total Material Cost	**$6.50**

If you don't know the cost of your goods yet, go online and find material costs to get a basic idea of pricing. When it's time to source the materials, you can get more accurate numbers.

Product Cost of Time

You need to understand the cost of time in creating and selling your product or service.

Estimate how long it takes you to create the product and multiply it by your hourly rate to get the manpower cost. Add that to your Total Material Cost to get your **Break Even** product price. If you don't plan to cover your time, use Total Material Cost as your Break Even product price. If you want to make a profit, you shouldn't sell it for less than your Break Even price.

MATERIAL	REQUIRED	PRICE	TOTAL COST
Time	30 minutes	$15/hour	$7.50

Product Price Points for Profit

Create a product pricing table that includes your full **Retail Price**, a few sale price points and your Break Even price. Then, subtract the Break Even price you just calculated, from each retail price below, to see the potential profit at each price point.

	PRICE	BREAK EVEN	PROFIT
Retail	$9.99	$6.50	$3.49
10% Off Promo	$8.99	$6.50	$2.49
20% Off Promo	$7.99	$6.50	$1.49
Break Even	$6.50	$6.50	$0.00

Product Transaction & Listing Fees

If you are selling online or accepting credit cards, there will also be **transaction** or **processing fees** which are deducted based on the order total. These fees are usually about $0.30 plus 3% of the total transaction. If you sell something for $10, $0.60 will be kept by the platform (like Etsy, PayPal or Square) and you will receive $9.40. For $100, $3.30 goes to the platform while you keep $96.70. Therefore; you should estimate putting aside 4-6% for fees. The cheaper your product, the higher the percentage you should use in your calculations for fees.

Online marketplaces where you can sell your item may charge listing fees. In our example, let's assume your marketplace charges $0.20 for listing your product for a three-month duration. Guestimate how long your product will need to be listed before it is sold. Do you think your item will sell in three months or will it need to be relisted and incur a second listing fee?

Update your pricing table to include any fees.

	PRICE	FEES	BREAK EVEN	PROFIT
Retail	$9.99	$.80	$6.50	$2.69
10% Off Promo	$8.99	$.77	$6.50	$1.72
20% Off Promo	$7.99	$.74	$6.50	$0.75
Break Even	$6.50	$.70	$6.50	- $.70

Uh oh! As you can see, selling your product at the Break Even point won't work unless you've factored in all other costs associated with selling your product.

Product Sales Goals

Now let's talk about goal setting. Let's say a teddy bear artisan wants to bring in an extra $100 a month. How many teddy bears does she need to sell?

To figure this out, take the $100 goal and divide it by each price point's profit. If you're calculating a number with a decimal, round up to the next number. (You can't sell .25 of a bear!)

	PRICE	FEES	BREAK EVEN	PROFIT
Retail	$9.99	$.80	$6.50	$2.69
10% Off Promo	$8.99	$.77	$6.50	$1.72
20% Off Promo	$7.99	$.74	$6.50	$0.75
Break Even	$6.50	$.70	$6.50	- $.70

# of Sold Bears	38	59	134	N/A

Can you now see how pricing severely impacts your bottom line and your business' overall success? Just because something appears to have a minimal cost, doesn't mean its value is defined in the same way.

PLAN FOR PROFIT

Now that you know how to calculate and appropriately price products to turn a profit, you can also calculate whether you can make money with your business.

Selling 30 bears in one month doesn't mean you get to take home that $100. It depends on how you plan to legally establish your business and also expenses to run your business. **Expenses** include things you purchase that are not based on the finished product like equipment, office supplies, marketing, booth fees, subscriptions, hosting, rent and licenses.

List out all of the items that you think you will need to pay for each month.

ITEM	COST
Hosting	$5.00
Marketing	$20.00
Equipment	$12.00
Total	$37.00

While you made $100 net profit off the sale of your bears, $37 of that is needed to pay your overhead costs. If you want to make a **monthly gross profit** of $100 then you will need to adjust your product sale goals to accommodate your **estimated monthly expenses**. In our teddy bear case, we'd estimate $50 a month in expenses, needing to sell 45 teddy bears at the retail price to bring home our goal $100.

Prepared to earn a profit?

Now that you have completed these exercises and have numbers to guide you, take the time to reflect and answer this question: "Can I handle my business?"

Can you see yourself raising your prices or negotiating lower-priced materials to increase your profits?

Can you commit to the hours that are required? In our example, it would take someone 22.5 hours a month, to create the product, which doesn't include managing the business, shipping and interacting with customers.

This question is not meant to discourage you from starting a business. I just want you to have a clear vision of what your business needs so that you have confidence in knowing that you will make a profit. If you can't make these numbers work or if you can't imagine asking people to pay a price that brings you enough profit, you may need to reassess. Is this business really the right choice for you and your family? Can you live with yourself if you charge more?

Self-worth is a complicated topic. Too many times I've seen mompreneurs give up because of challenges with prices and profit. The advice I give everyone is quite simple:

Don't charge what YOU would be willing to pay.

Keep in mind your ideal client, what would SHE pay for your unique personality, point of view and product? Be realistic, of course, but don't associate the product price with your personal worth.

If you're selling an eBook for $3.99, that doesn't mean the hours you invested writing and designing it (or the years of experience it took to gain the wisdom shared within it) are only worth that much. That is just what the market will bear. And, on a similar note, giving your eBook away for free (to grow your email list) doesn't make its value any less either

Just because one person says, "No," to your product's pricing doesn't mean you need to make reductions. Instead, keep your perfect customer in mind and go after them!

PLAN FOR NETWORK MARKETING

No matter your business, I believe every entrepreneur should be involved with a network marketing company. Good network marketing companies provide you with the products, tools and training you need, so that you can get out there and work your business. This allows you to exercise and practice the other parts of running a business, mainly connecting with your prospective customers and working on your personal brand or business style. The sales training they provide can usually be applied to your own business and you are automatically plugged into a vast network of other like-minded individuals.

Take a look at the network marketing companies out there, sample their products, listen to their pitches and choose the one that works best as a companion to your business. By picking one that complements your business, you can potentially cross-sell your clients. For example: a yoga instructor would find essential oils or candles complementary and could cross sell them to her yoga students and yoga to her network marketing or direct sales customers.

For a mompreneur, a network marketing business can help diversify your revenue streams and create residual income. I've worked at network marketing corporate offices and participated in them as consultants too. I truly believe it's an industry that can be beneficial to a lot of people—if you do it the right way. Network marketing is not a get-rich-quick scheme as you still have to put in the time and energy to make it a business and not a hobby. This is just another reason of many for why I think practice with a networking marketing business is a helpful idea. Best of all, the profits can be used to pay off the startup costs of your own business!

STEP 5: ESTABLISH

You will save yourself a lot of headaches down the road, by spending time now in researching different types of business structures. It's important to reach out to professionals for advice and help. Like everything in life, there is no perfect or best solution; there are simply options for different needs and situations. I recommend contacting an accountant or attorney to get an idea of which tax structure will work for you, so that you are clear on the advantages of choosing one option over another.

If you don't have an accountant or attorney, it is time for you to ask around for referrals. You don't want to have to shop for a lawyer upon getting served; and for sure, you don't want to look for an accountant during their busiest time of year! Reach out to your network, check with your local Chamber of Commerce, or ask your online business groups for recommendations. Meet with these professionals in person so that you can get a feel for them and ask any and all questions you have. Bring a list of your questions, so that you can ask the same questions of each person and more accurately gauge their responses and advice. Believe me, having a lawyer's number in your available contacts brings peace of mind—even if you never have to use them or opt for a self-guided, online document service like LegalZoom.

Personally, I recommend hiring an accountant as they can usually process business filings as well as accounting, tax prep and payroll services. It's a worthwhile expense to invest in your business to save yourself the headaches that can go along with doing it all yourself. I love being in control of my finances, but as a business owner, it's time to let go and delegate. Letting a professional handle the complicated stuff allows you to focus on your art, product and customers. You may not need an accountant all the time, but reaching out to one to discuss your business structure will set you up in the best possible way for your business and family tax returns. If you are interested in doing research on your own, visit the Small Business Association at SBA.gov. It's a great resource for information and events.

ESTABLISH YOUR BUSINESS

There are several business structures from which you can choose to establish your business. Research each of your options (and be sure to seek professional advice) to see which one will suit your business as it grows from infancy into adulthood.

Creating a **sole proprietorship** is the most simple and common type of business to establish. It is owned and run by one person with no distinction between the business and the owner. You get all of the profits, however; you are also responsible for all of the business debts, losses and liabilities. This is the most basic business structure and easy one to establish. If you are a freelancer, photographer or artist, or you deposit payments for sold goods in your personal bank account, then you already have a sole proprietorship!

A **partnership** is like a sole proprietorship except there is more than one owner and you share responsibility in the business profits or losses. Each partner contributes to the business in some way, such as investment of money, time, or experience, and each partner shares in the business profits or losses. Partnerships can get tricky when it comes to decision-making. You'll want a clear understanding of how the business will be managed.

Business filings will define how much each partner owns of the company, but you should have a partnership agreement in place that clarifies each partner's role, duties and division of profits. It should also delineate how losses or debit will be managed, how disputes will be resolved and how to dissolve the partnership—if required. You must have these hard talks now and put everything in writing. Depending on your local laws, a partnership agreement may or may not be required to establish the business, however; it is extremely risky to operate a business without one—especially if you are partners with family or friends!

If you want to conduct business under a different name than your legal name then you should look into filing a **Fictitious Business Name (FBN)** with your local government. There are usually fees associated with the filing and some sort of public notice or publication requirement. Visit your city, county and state web site or local municipal building to get specific information that applies to your business and local area.

More advanced business structures include **limited liability corporations (LLC)** or **partnership (LLP)** and **corporations** which allow you to separate your business from yourself. There are usually more expensive fees associated with establishing and maintaining these types of business structures. Each has different requirements and specific ways of reporting taxes based on various ownership models. An LLC can be owned by a sole proprietor; an LLP can be owned by partners with a split of the company defined by a percentage; and a corporation is owned by shareholders, usually managed by a board of directors.

There are complexities, benefits and tax consequences for each business structure so I recommend reaching out to a local professional, such as an accountant, business manager or lawyer to provide you specific advice for your unique situation, business and goals.

Here are some questions to ask yourself (and a qualified professional), when establishing your business:

- Who owns the company?

- What are the financial circumstances of the business owner(s)?
- Who runs the company?
- How are decisions made for the company?
- Who works for the company? How many employees does the company have?
- How will the financial books be kept?
- How much money is the business projected to make each year?
- How much will be paid out in expenses each year?
- What is the long-term plan for the business?
- Where will the business be located?
- Who will be paying the start-up costs?
- What processes will be in place to track incidental expenses and mileage?
- Is the product or service the business is providing regulated? If so, what additional requirements and fees need to be considered?
- Will special insurance be necessary?

ESTABLISH YOUR BOARD

There is excitement in the notion of working for ourselves, not letting someone else boss us around and setting our own schedules. Let me lay it out for you: entrepreneurs have bosses—the business is our boss. We do whatever it takes to keep the boss content and the business humming. Yes, we can skip a few Fridays or work from the beach some days, but it also means we've worked countless nights and more than a few weekends and vacations prior.

*"I don't work for myself,
I work for my business."*

Peta Kelly, PetaKelly.com

As a CEO of a corporation with several divisions, managed by me, myself and I, it can be complicated knowing which master to serve at what time. To help me manage the chaos, I came up with an exercise called the Mental Board Meeting. I especially like this exercise as I can get very artistic at times. I get a vision in my head of what I want to create and go full steam ahead. With the use of my mental board, I can manage what I invest my time in, instead of diving straight into a project or task without boundaries.

Exercise: Mental Board Meeting

Close your eyes and imagine a large table with several versions of yourself sitting around it. (Remember Pixar's animated film, "Inside Out"? Kind of like that.) Consider these versions of yourself as 'Yous'. At this meeting there is the CEO You, who runs the show, HR You, who keeps all of the other 'Yous' in line, 'Accountant You', who makes sure you can pay bills and make money, as well as 'Mom You', 'Wife You', and 'Self You' who all deserve a seat at the table too. (If you have more than one business venture, invite a 'You' for each business to this meeting.)

When you are first starting out, you don't need to have all of these 'Yous' on your Mental Board: a CEO, Creator and a Money Gal are a great start. Your Boss or Chief Executive Officer alter ego should care most about the health of the business. The 'CEO You', looks out for the business's best interests—not yours. The 'Creator You' is your Chief Passion Officer— she fights for your passions and interests, and is fueled by your 'Why'. She wants to give as much of you as she can to the world. You can also think of her as your Chief Production Officer. She is the one who takes action, creates, builds and executes everything that is needed for the business. Your Money Gal or Chief Financial Officer is all about the numbers. If numbers and money talk aren't your thing, then just have your Money Gal ask questions during meetings to challenge you to provide answers. "Who will pay for that? How will that make money? How will we reach that goal? How can we reduce those costs?"

The purpose of your Mental Board of Directors is to help you navigate difficult decisions and situations. For each 'You' that attends your meetings, imagine all of their attributes—think of their position and how they would feel, act, talk and even dress. Then, let them take the floor of the board meeting. Each 'You', gets a chance to share and 'CEO You' gets the final say.

Don't be surprised if you are given guidance during your meeting. Your subconscious (or the divine) may reveal an idea, choice or decision which could help you in your current situation.

STEP 6: BUILD

By completing the previous steps and their exercises, you should have a clear understanding of your brand. The foundation is now set for you to build your business! This next step can feel daunting, as there may be many things you need to get done and you may not know how to do all of it. It's okay to feel overwhelmed, and out of your element. It's part of the entrepreneurial journey! What separates the entrepreneur from 'wantrepreneur' is this step: execution. All the planning and designing means nothing if you don't take action and make it happen.

"You can have a to do list... but are you doing it?
Or are you just showing off your
'Busy Mom' badge?"

Laurie Joy, TheMojoMama.com

Exercise: To Do List

Before you start building, let's make a list of everything you'll need to create to launch your business. Don't filter yourself or start categorizing or prioritizing. Set a timer for 10-15 minutes and write down everything you can possibly think of that needs to get done. Here are some items to help get you started...

- Website
- Logo
- Photoshoot
- File DBA
- Bank Account
- Business phone number
- Set up social media accounts
- Order materials
- Create prototype or samples
- Packaging
- Business cards
- Postcards
- Booth props
- City business licenses
- Domain name
- Set up emails
- Research online payment options PayPal®
- Write content
- Mailing list
- Opt-in offer

I love to make these lists on sticky notes, so after I write them all out, I can reorganize them by time frame or importance. You can also use Google Docs to create a list or better yet, a spreadsheet to track, categorize, schedule and report on your tasks. Order things first by dependency and importance. For instance, you can't get a bank account without having your DBA, so your bank account is dependent upon you completing the DBA. As you organize, more tasks will come to mind, so add them to your list.

When you feel comfortable with the order of the list, go through it again and do the exercise again for each task, creating and prioritizing subtasks. For instance 'Web Site' would include sub tasks like…

- Hire designer
- Write content
- Build site
- Launch site
- Purchase hosting
- Select platform
- Test site

- Site features

While 'Open bank account' may just include…

- Research Banks
- Save enough for opening deposit

Continue breaking each task into subtasks until they feel more manageable and not so daunting to you. Writing them out clears some space in your mind, documents them for others and makes you accountable with yourself to actually DO them! Doing this exercise takes you from, "I'm going insane, I have so much to do!" to "I've got a handle on this and I know exactly what I need to focus on right now!" Bravo to you!

The rest of this chapter is focused on providing guidance for items you may have on your task list. As each business is different, each item is listed alphabetically and not based on priority. What is most important to my businesses may not be as important to yours.

EMAIL

There are lots of options out there to provide you email service, however the most important is to be able to use your own domain. If you own your own domain name, you should also be able to get an email address with it. For example, using yourbusinessname@gmail.com doesn't look as professional as hello@successfulmompreneur.com.

If you like using Gmail to access, read and send your emails, you can either use Google Business Apps or use Gmail's "Check Other Email I Own" feature.

Hosting companies will sell you separate email services, or, if you have cPanel hosting, it includes an email system and allows many email boxes, aliases and also domain forwards. Don't be afraid to call your hosting company (or ones you are researching) and ask them questions. Most will help you get set up, just be careful about the costs of upgrades and features you may not be looking for your email service at this time.

If you want multiple email addresses you need to decide what you want them to do. If you want to receive and send mail from the email address, you'll need to create an email account, such as hello@successfulmompreneur.com. If you just want to receive email from it, but not send from it, then you can set up an alias to have it delivered to another account you plan to send from. For example, create an alias for events@successfulmompreneur.com which be an alias for the main account, Hello. This is also good for generic emails like hello@, info@, events@, or sales@, which you will usually post publicly online so that you don't offer your name or personal email. An alias is also good for supporting multiple versions of your name. While your email account may be Jenn@, you can have an alias of Jennifer@ or Jen@ to ensure you receive emails even if someone mistypes your address. Domain forwards are useful if you have multiple domain names and want to accept emails from both.

EMAIL SIGNATURE

Add another level of professionalism with a branded email signature. Keep it simple with the basic info like phone, email and domain name but ensure it fits your branding standards. You can include your photo or logo for a memorable touch but depending on your recipient's settings, sometimes images don't automatically display.

Some platforms like Gmail have a **what you see is what you get** (**WYSIWYG**) feature allowing you to copy and paste a signature that you created in Word or Google Docs, while others require the email signature to be formatted in HTML. In those cases, you can design the email signatures you in want in Word or Google Docs, then save it as HTML, open in the Notepad app to copy and paste the source code.

MAILING LISTS

No matter your business, you need a mailing list! It's your most consistent way to market and communicate with your prospects and customers. Simply publishing a new blog article doesn't mean your readers will visit and read it. Social networking feeds are controlled by algorithms to support users and paying sponsors—there is no guarantee that your posts will be seen by your fans. Therefore, an email campaign sent to your mailing list has a higher chance of being delivered and viewed. There are still the obstacles of junk folders, spam settings and unread emails, yet it's more in your control than the other communication tools out there.

Your mailing list is a database of anyone who has shown enough interest in your company and product to provide you their email address. You can build your mailing list directly from your web site, have a piece of paper or tablet at your booth or brick and mortar register. When you are at networking events, instead of giving out your contact info, ask for theirs. When someone asks for your business card, hand it to them and ask if they'd like to stay up to date with new product launches, promos or events. When they say yes, get them on your list. Ask them to follow you on your social networking sites too—but your mailing list is the most important. A 'Follow' or 'Like' in social media is the least amount of commitment a person can make and doesn't usually lead to a sale. Constant communication to a warm lead through email marketing can.

You can write campaigns to be info-rich newsletters or short conversations, like you'd send to a friend. The style and frequency depends solely on your brand and your commitment to constancy.

There are plenty of mass mailing systems out there, some free and some paid, all with similar basic features and then some unique bells and whistles. I recommend that WordPress clients start with MailChimp as there are many plugins that quickly integrate an opt-in subscription into a WordPress site. WordPress also has a user-friendly interface for importing, managing, designing and sending campaigns. Plus, its use is free for up to

2,000 subscribers, which is not a bad a place to start!

When you send email campaigns, you need to be aware of the general aspects of email laws for your business. At the time of writing this book, in the United States the CAN-SPAM Act sets the rules for commercial email which defines requirements for commercial email messages and gives recipients the right to opt out of receiving emails. When you set up your MailChimp or other mass mailing provider account it will ask you to provide your information, such as a physical mailing address, so you can be compliant with current laws when you send your email campaigns. Some will require double opt-in, meaning a person subscribes to your website and is then sent a confirmation email that they must click before completing the subscription processes.

Some mailing list platforms have schedules where you can send emails after specific timeframes or actions. You are trying to connect these warm leads into returning customers, so don't throw everything at them all at once. Spreading your messages out keeps your business and products in mind without overflowing their mailbox. For some businesses, one email a month is a sweet spot, while for others it's once a week, or even more frequently for events or holiday promotions. It's your brand and your choice—just be mindful and consistent.

MAILING LIST OPT-IN OFFER

When someone subscribes to your email list, you can reward them with a free offer or promotion. Most offers I use involve providing relevant and useful info in the form of a PDF, video or webinar. The PDF can be an eBook, checklist, blueprint, Top 10 list, worksheet or printable. It can even be a template in a Google Doc or spreadsheet. Maybe it's an invite to a secret Facebook Group, or your offer could be access to a live or recorded online live event, video, podcast or series. It could be one video or a series. It could be a podcast or other downloadable content like a song, meditation or even artwork. This freebie can be on the confirmation page of your mailing subscription, included in the welcome email sent to the new subscriber, or both!

No matter what you choose, it should provide value to your subscriber. This is your chance to show off what you can do for them. This is a taste of your awesomeness before they buy. Don't give away the farm—but don't be stingy and give them something worthless. You're better off not providing an offer than giving away a useless one that could do more harm than good.

PHOTOGRAPHY

By now, you have spent a lot of time on planning your brand to present your business as professional and constant. Unfortunately, I've seen too many clients invest thousands of dollars in their business and then use poor photography—or even selfies—for their bio photo.

All of your photographs for your products, headshot and lifestyle photos, need to be on point with your branding. Your photos are the quickest way a prospect can become intrigued with your product. These are the surest way for them to have an emotional reaction and be motivated to read further and purchase.

Great photography doesn't mean you always have to hire a pro. For product photos, you can make a simple lightbox at home and use a point and click or even a smartphone camera. The better the lighting and original photo, the less retouching or color correction you will need to do. There are countless tutorials on photography that the web can give you for step-by-step, how-to photography directions.

However, for your headshot or lifestyle photos of yourself, hire a pro. If you can't afford one, reach out and see if they would be interested in a trade of some kind. If not, reach out to a friend or family member whose photos of other people on Instagram always look good. Or, head over to a studio at the mall. I can't stress enough that selfies, pics of you with your kids, or you in your wedding dress or maternity shoot are not appropriate choices for your business bio photo. Those are great lifestyle or 'My Story' photos but shouldn't be used to show who the face of your company is— even if you sell wedding dresses or provide childcare. Your bio photo is the first impression many of your prospects will get of you. It should be authentically you while coming across as a trusted authority in your field.

For lifestyle photos, you can purchase rights to images at iStock Photo, Adobe, Creative Market and many other stock or royalty-free photography sites. Most sites allow you to download a proof of the photo to see how it will look placed on your site or print piece. Don't buy until you are sure it works in your project and with your brand. Also try to purchase it at the best price by using Google's Image search. You can upload the proof image and Google will display similar image results where you may be able to purchase the file at a lower price. It will also show you other companies that have already used it. You'll probably want to rethink any images that a competitor is already using. If you don't want to run the risk of that in the future, you'll probably need to have your own lifestyle photoshoot.

For any photoshoot you do, research the types of photos you want, by either sharing a Pinterest board with your photographer or providing a shot list or storyboards. Be upfront and share with your photographer how you plan to use the photos, how many locations you need and any outfit changes you'll require. This will help you and your photographer figure out accurate pricing for what is needed. For example, you won't need a print credit in your photography package if the photos are all going to be used online. Orientation is also different for web vs. print, so this information will be helpful for your photographer to have. They will need to determine which shots should be orientated for portrait (tall, thin photos) or vs. landscape (short, wide photos). For web site backgrounds, landscape photos with wide backgrounds work and the subject (either you or product) one one-third of photo work best to provide interest and room for copy on the other two-thirds side.

PRINT MARKETING

Business cards aren't as prevalent in our digital age, but still a necessity for many businesses. If you are on the fence about needing them, do this fun visualization exercise. Imagine randomly meeting your perfect customer at a playground, in line at a theme park, at the grocery store, at your day job, or wherever you make a connection, sharing each other's stories and…they ask you for more information. What do you do? In your mind's eye, do you hand them a business card? Get out your phone to swap numbers or do you become Facebook friends? Do you hand them a pocket brochure? Scribble your number on a napkin? What reaction do you think will be the most effective at convincing them to reach out and visit your site, make a purchase or call for an appointment?

Try to make the decision based on the reaction you want from your perfect customer and not on assumptions about the costs associated with getting them printed.

Today, there are a lot of printing options out there for you! You can design your own marketing items, upload your design files or customize a pre-designed option online at Staples, VistaPrint, Moo or OvernightPrints. Each print-on-demand company usually offers different sizes, paper quality and thickness, finishes and shipping rates. Staples even has a same-day service for when you are in a bind or that special opportunity arises! If you order online, do a quick search for promo codes at RetailMeNot, Groupon or similar coupon or promo code sit—every dollar saved counts!

Brochures can convey more information about your business and may be given more attention than a business card. Their size alone demands more immediate attention—even if stuffed into a diaper bag. When designing the brochure, try to be balanced. Too many paragraphs of copy and it will be boring. Too many photos without copy may look good but may not provide enough value or information. Text should be easy to read, with clear headlines, paragraph copy and bullet points to break up large blocks of text. A photo can immediately convey a feeling, idea or product. If you are using stock or royalty-free photos, check the licensing agreement, there is usually a limit to the print quantity.

Postcards are another option to use instead of business cards, as they act as a hybrid between brochure and business card. The 4" x 6" postcards are standard but jumbo 11" x 6" are more noticeable when they arriving in the mailbox. If you plan on using them as mailers, be sure to leave space for postage and postal barcodes when designing them. Most online design programs like VistaPrint should warn you of the space that should be left blank for postal requirements.

Personally, I like to use business cards for one-on-one situations where I want to connect with the person I'm speaking with. I use postcards for product specific images and guide them to the web site for more info. This way I can hand them out at shows, and leave them on bulletin boards in places where I don't feel comfortable providing my phone number to just anyone.

PRODUCTS

In the previous steps you thought about your designs, pricing and maybe even created a prototype. Now you need to finalize and start creating your products!

Are you selling a service?

A **service** is when a customer exchanges money for your time and not for a physical product. Examples of services include: photography, coaching, web design, child care, gardening, dog walking, book keeping, etc.

When providing a service, managing contracts, tracking your time, and invoicing will probably be the most important aspects of running your business. Thankfully, there are a lot of options on the market to support you, so you don't have to figure it out on your own. Talk with your accountant and lawyer to see what they recommend for your business, especially when it comes to payroll and contracts. For example, you can choose accounting software like QuickBooks for invoices or online tools like 17 Hats. If you have a WordPress website you can even use special plugins like Sprouts Invoices that track time spent on projects and allows customers to pay invoices online.

Setting everything up and running a test of your whole intake process from start to finish (including lead generation, contract signing, payment, service and even follow-up thank yous) before your first client will work out any kinks and give you enough experience to get through any jitters. After you test it yourself, have a friend or favorite client run through it as well. Ask for feedback on any steps that felt awkward for them. If you can't improve it (maybe it's a feature of the invoicing system you are using), see about providing instructions to clarify steps that will help you guide your customers through the process more easily.

Are you selling digital goods?

A **digital product** is something that a customer purchases and is delivered online. It can include things like eBooks, checklists, webinars, printables, tutorials and patterns, artwork, photos, music and anything else you can dream up! Digital products are wonderful at creating residual income, as they let you work smarter not harder. You create the product once and can sell it an unlimited amount of times which makes for great profit. Automated delivery, payment methods and security will most likely be important aspects of your business.

There are industry specific sites that have been created for your unique needs. Banzoogle.com is good for musicians or other artists with audio recordings like meditations. PixelSet and SmugMug support the display and sale of photos. Print-on-demand manufactures like Zazzle or Studio6 let artists create and sell graphic designs on everything from canvas to mugs to shoes. iStock and CreativeMarket let graphic designers sell clipart, fonts and photos. Etsy is great for sewing patterns and tutorials. Some of these sites even have widgets or plugins that you can add to your website so that you can sell or cross-advertise products.

Another way to deliver digital goods is through a membership site. Customers purchase a monthly or yearly membership and get access to a library of digital resources. Security plays a bigger part here as you want to minimize people sharing passwords or downloading and distributing your content. At the very least, include rules and regulations in your purchase agreement or terms of use. There are plenty of plugins and platforms you can use to add membership security to your site. In my experience, I have found WPMUdev's WordPress plugin suite to be highly flexible for memberships.

If selling individual digital goods, a link to the file should exist on the on-screen receipt as well as the emailed receipt. You will need to decide if you want to limit the number of times a digital download can occur. An automated delivery system like WPMUdev's Marketplace accepts payments and sends a customized link to buyers, which means you can virtually make money in your sleep!

Are you selling physical goods?

A **physical product** is something that will be delivered to the customer either shipped from a site or hand-delivered through a store or booth. It can be anything you can imagine—if you can hold it or touch it, it's a physical good.

Be sure to check with your local government regarding your specific services or products. In addition to tax responsibilities you should be aware of, there may be specific regulations, licenses or certifications your business needs before you can begin selling products. For example, if you are a therapist, architect or accountant, you will probably need certification, or, if you are selling food products, your kitchen may need to be inspected.

PRODUCT PACKAGING AND DISPLAY

While the saying, "Don't judge a book by its cover," may be true, keep in mind that the cover, or the package, may be the first glimpse of your product.

An item's appearance is extremely important with physical goods. The way a box looks, how kits are bagged, price tags and product signage are what draw a customer into your booth or store. Successfully coordinating these things together can convey a level of trust, stability and longevity to your buyers.. Ensure your brand shines through and keep in mind your price points. If you are selling designer, high-end jewelry, handmade signs can convey more of a garage sale feel than one of luxury.

Even with digital products, you can still create packaging. Mp3 files need album artwork. eBooks can be mocked up online to look like printed books with a cover and spine. Digital downloads or videos can be mocked up as CDs or DVDs. These mockups are intended to show the buyer the content they are getting in visual terms for an instant, favorable impression. Beware though: don't create a false impression! If you are selling a 10-page, PDF eBook, don't use an image of a book with a thick spine and hundreds of pages. You don't want your buyer frustrated, feeling that they purchased more than they received.

PRODUCT SHIPPING

If you don't know your shipping costs, you run the risk of losing money when you ship orders. Invest in a scale so that you use accurate weights when purchasing postage online. Weigh the finished product (in its packaging) with the mailer or box you intend to ship it in. Some sites like Etsy allow you to create a shipping profile so that you can set a category of products to have the same mailing dimensions, rate and size.

Standardizing your shipping materials means less overhead and storage. Soft items like clothing can be shipped in thin plastic bags which can fit large items or be folded over to fit smaller items. Bubble mailers come in multiple sizes and should be used for items like CDs, DVDs and books. Boxes with tissue should be used for fragile items. Mock up a package, weigh it and use a postage calculator to get the idea of base shipping costs. In your shipping calculations, also include the cost of box, filling, labels or other shipping supplies.

Check multiple carrier options and rates. The USPS has a Priority package option which delivers in 1-3 days to most of the U.S. The boxes are free and some have flat-rate prices—great for filling with heavy items or multiple item orders. Also keep an eye for out for postage increases that usually happen in January and July each year. Otherwise, you may find yourself spending your hard-earned profits on extra shipping costs.

SEO: SEARCH ENGINE OPTIMIZATION

It's important to keep SEO, or Search Engine Optimization, in mind when writing your content for your site and blog. Your site is meant to educate visitors but should also pull in new people from web searches. Writing keyword-rich copy serves both the search engines and your readers. You can start off with a catchy, keyword stuffed title and then write the copy, or you can write your article and edit it afterward to add keywords.

Witty titles in your content may be attention-getters, but without the right keywords they can be vague and unsuccessful at landing organic search visitors.

The correct use of headlines will help with search results. Using your blog editor's **headline tags** (either labeled as Headline1 or H1 , H2, H3, etc.) how importance and precedence for both search engine bots (the programs that read your site and index it for future searches) and the reader. There should only be one H1 tag, usually the title of your page or blog article. The words in your H1 tag are given the most importance by search engines because it includes the topics and keywords that will be covered in more detail throughout the website. You can have several H2 tags, as these are used for sections or subtitles of your copy and are given more importance than regular paragraph text or H3 tags (yet still less important than H1 tags). Be sure to include your target keywords in the H2 tags, as well as your paragraph copy. The more those words show up, the better your ranking becomes with search results.

For example: "Black is the new White" may seem like a cool page title or headline, but from a search engine perspective, it doesn't provide enough specific, relevant to appear well in results. For a visitor searching for a web site, does the title convey what the article is about? Paint color? Photography? Fashion? A successful headline full of keywords to drive traffic to a fashion site would look like this: "Wedding Dress Color Trend: Black is the new White."

Image search is gaining importance and is not as complex as you might think. The first step is to give images descriptive names. Instead of logo.gif, I use successful-mompreneur-logo.gif. Be sure to use dashes instead of underscores to separate words, as search engines translate dashes into spaces which assists with search indexing. Pictures of yourself or your products require keyword rich file names. Don't just upload Img_3862.jpg direct from your camera; instead, upload and name the file jennifer-colucci-2017-spring-book-launch.jpg. These descriptive file names also help boost your business's Pins on Pinterest as it searches both file names (which you control) and the pin message (which is provided by the pinner). When adding the image to your sites, be sure it has an appropriate alternative text title (or alt tag). When a person accesses your site without seeing images, they can read the alt tag to know what the image may contain. This is also how search engine bots see your site, so it's another great place to add your targeted keywords.

There are free tools online to grade your site for SEO. They will provide you checklists of things you should do to improve your rankings such as having a sitemap, security certificate and tips for responsive design. You can Google search, "Check Site SEO", to learn more or use sites like, SEO Site Checkup, SEO Analyzer, SEO Checker, Varvy and Nibbler.

A site map is a page that lists all the links on your web site in one place so people and search engines can see them all at once. Think of it like a directory at a mall. Everything is listed in one place so that you don't have to figure out where in the navigation something should be found. Search engines like to see a site have both a user-friendly site map as well as an XML version for themselves. Some platforms like WordPress have built-in site maps or plugins that will generate both versions for you.

Responsive sites are designed in a way that no matter the device you use to view the web site, i.e. large format monitor, laptop, tablet or mobile, your web site automatically optimizes to show the best version of itself. That may mean a site that has three side-by-side columns on a laptop reorganizes itself to be one column stacked on top of each other when viewed via tablet or cell phone. The good news is that most platforms now understand the importance of responsive design in today's market and provide it to their customers, but you should remain aware that not all of them do. It is best to both check your site via mobile for layout issues and/or have the expectation that your design may not look the best on your customer's mobile devices.

A security certificate provides **Secure Socket Layer** (**SSL**) encryption for data sent to and from your site. It is required for ecommerce sites and highly recommended for sites that transmit personal data like passwords and other identifiable information. Certificates cost $20-$100+ a year, and provide peace of mind to your customers. Platforms like WordPress will need to be configured to default to HTTPS for logins and other relevant pages.

SOCIAL NETWORKS

Social sites can be important tools for your business, but keep in mind they are not the only way to attract customers. Each platform: Facebook, Instagram, Twitter, Pinterest, LinkedIn, etc., all have different ways to present your business and connect with a specific audience. While you don't have to be on every social site, you do have to create a presence where your target customers exists. Simply creating profiles on social sites is not enough. You will need to engage with your account and audience (including prospects and not just your followers), so that you can be relevant and grow. Your intent with social networking should be to grow for a specific reason or business goal. Getting 3,000 fans or followers means nothing to your bottom line if you don't have a strategy to convert them into email subscribers and repeat customers.

Facebook is usually the main social media network your business should have. It allows a lot of different content to be shared, from short messages to long notes, an individual photo to photo albums, events, polls and sale posts. You can create a Facebook Page for people to Like which then means your posts will show on their newsfeed, depending on Facebook's current algorithm. If you aren't ready to build your own web site, a Facebook Page can stand in its place while you get started. You can also create a Facebook Group, either open or secret, and invite people to join and participate by posting and engaging with other group members. Groups are great for coaches, network marketing teams and other businesses where you are building a community.

Instagram is used for sharing images; primarily lifestyle photos. Typical ads are not welcome here! There is a unique art to advertising on Instagram, so be sure to study up on your favorite brands or even your greatest competitor for ideas. Instagrammers aren't looking for your professional-looking, marketing shots of your products. They want to see real-life uses of your products, behind-the-scenes glimpses at the making of your product, or even glimpses into the inner workings of your business and employees' work habits. employees. Depending on the nature of your business, you can choose to either create a business account or share images under on your personal account. Some strategists recommend that you link your Instagram account to Facebook so that your Instagram posts can be automatically shared at the same time with both audiences. This can help with analytics, however; it all depends on your business's overall marketing strategy. Some companies prefer to share different images on different social sites, and/or choose to stagger the timing of posts.

Twitter allows you to share short messages or images with a broad audience. Twitter is most often used by companies vs. individuals. This is especially true being that its primary audience (18-25 years old) has shifted over to new platforms like SnapChat. Although it is no longer as popular a tool for reaching out to individuals, it is still a good presence to have, as it allows businesses to reach out and network with each other for creative, community-based marketing campaigns. As with Instagram, you can enable your Facebook posts to automatically Tweet to your Twitter audience, thereby creating an active presence on Twitter with minimal effort (though formatting issues may occur.) You can also enable Instagram photos to automatically Tweet as well.

Pinterest allows people to save inspirational images to different pin boards. While it is widely used and reported to increase return on investment more than other social sites, there is minimal engagement that actually occurs on the pins. It's main use is to attract users to click through the pins to your web site or blog posts.

LinkedIn is focused on social networking for businesses and professionals. Businesses can create a corporate account to share information about the company for use with connecting employees, industry professionals or recruits. If your business provides services to other businesses, it is a good place to for you to create a presence.

Google+ is different from other social networks as it focuses more on interest communities. You don't need to be connected to someone to be able to interact, as you can engage with others who share similar interests. As it is a Google product, there is a benefit to having your business on Google, being that it helps improve your search rankings and increases your reach beyond your other social network followers.

Search for 'demographics of social networking' to view usage reports on how social media is used by different age groups and audiences. This may be of help when trying to figure out the best place to invest your time in reaching your ideal customer.

WEB SITE

Yes, you can do it yourself! Technology has come a long way and there are many different options now for DIYers or those on a budget. The trick is to understand that you get what you pay for.

Begin by making a list of the pages and features you want for your web site. Every site should have an About page, Contact Form, and a Products or Services section. These can either all be included on one long, scrolling page or placed on separate pages. From there, people can click to other sections including categories, photo galleries, products/product details, testimonials, more lead forms and a portfolio.

Features of your web site may involve more than just content and usually have specific functions that display data as well as content. Some features to consider are a contact form, blog, search, ecommerce, mailing list opt-ins, forums, invoices, memberships, protected content, appointment scheduling, calculators, listings, etc. When you make your feature list, prioritize it based on what is required for your launch vs. what you can add later. Use this list when you research DIY site platforms or when interviewing designers. By having a list, you will know the right site platform or design when you see it! Why pay a monthly fee for a site with a shopping cart if you never plan to sell things online? Or, if you plan to sell things online eventually, why start on a free platform that doesn't provide a way to upgrade so that you can sell things?

Be aware of hidden or upsell costs. The site may be free, but you may have to pay for an email and checkout system. Calculate the cost of all the upgrades or plugins you'll need from each platform you are researching so that you can compare apples to apples before making your final decision.

Some web site platform suggestions include: Wix, Weebly, SquareSpace, Virb or Shopify. While these platforms are user-friendly for the DIYer, I recommend a WordPress hosted solution. WordPress is a content management system, or CMS, with thousands of plugins (some for free, some for a fee) which allow you to customize your site to your heart's content. There are also thousands of different themes that automatically format and design your web site for you with just a few clicks. I recommend this to most of my clients so that they can have a website that scales (grows or shrinks) to suit their business needs, is portable (it can be moved from one hosting company to another) and is supported by many companies, developers and designers.

WEB SITE BLOG

Blogging keeps your website relevant and fresh for both your site visitors and search engines. There are multiple platforms for blogging and I recommend WordPress due to its flexibility for other website features. If you choose a blogging platform like Blogger, Tumblr, Medium, Ghost, SquareSpace, or Wix then use the domain name option for a more professional look. For example: JenniferColucci.com is better than JenniferColucci.BlogSpot.com. If you want to separate your blog from your main website you can do so with a **subdomain** (something that comes before your domain name) like blog.JenniferColucci.com or come up with a cute name that fits with your brand (like Honest Company's "Honestly" Blog.)

Create and stick to a writing schedule for your blog so that you can be consistent. Don't plan on writing once a day or once a week if you can't stay consistent. I recommend blogging at least once a month when you are first starting out. If you find yourself writing more, you can always increase your posts, but there is nothing worse than a blog with 2-3 posts per week for two weeks and then nothing for a year. This shows your readers that your priorities are elsewhere and makes it appear like things have gone stale or maybe even out of business.

Blogs don't have to be written the same day they are published! Most platforms let you schedule posts, so you can write several blogs and then schedule them throughout the week or month. When you are planning your schedule, set aside a few hours to write all of your blog posts so that you can schedule them out ahead of time.

WEB SITE CONTENT

Here's another option for you to DIY or hire a pro. Writing your own content for your website or printed marketing materials can seem scary but is also highly rewarding. If you choose to work with a copywriter, expect to provide them with your style guide and to participate in a few interviews so that they can understand the voice of your company.

Either way, you'll need to start out with an outline of the pages or sections you'll need to write. Just like your task list, go back to each item and break down any details you want to include. For example:

- Products
  - Name
  - Photo
  - Story
  - Price
  - Buy button
- About
  - Company
  - Product Benefits
  - Mission, Vision, Values
  - Charitable Donations
  - Founder's Story

- Education
- Passion
- Why I started the company
- Contact
  - Business Phone
  - Social Media Links
  - Email Form Fields
    - Name
    - Phone
    - Email
    - How'd You Hear About Us

You can hand this outline over to your writer or use it as a checklist for writing your own content. If you are doing the writing yourself, don't worry about writing the perfect first sentence. Take a random bullet point and write whatever you can think of for it. Do the same for the rest of the bullet points. Combine them all together, rearranging and editing until you have your web content! Send it off to a supportive friend who can proofread it for you and provide you with constructive criticism (ideally, find one who is similar to your ideal customer.) Try not to feel badly about their critiques. They may represent your audience and it's most important that they connect with the content you have provided.

STEP 7: SHARE

You've done all the planning, dreaming and creating—now it's time to share your business and your products with the world!

As the momma to this business baby, you'll need to take it out to play dates, socialize, show it off, and yes, even silently compare it to others.

Think you're not a good salesperson? Have you ever noticed when another woman compliments you on your clothes, shoes, etc., you say something like, "Thanks, I got it at…"? Well, us women are natural sharers. As moms, our share filter is reduced further (really, did you ever imagine you'd be sharing so many poop stories with people before having a kid?) And yet, for a lot of us, selling is hard. We fear rejection, looking pushy and turning so salesy that we lose friends.

It's okay, moms. You don't have to be a saleswoman to have a successful business. What you need to do is make connections with your ideal customers. Don't you love it when you walk into your favorite coffee shop or juice bar franchise location and they know you by name and your 'usual' order? Don't you prefer that location to others? The product is exactly the same, but the experience is different. You feel cared for and appreciated because they have connected with you—treating you like a person and not just the next latte in a long line of lattes. You are more than just another empty cup waiting to be filled, and your prospective customers feel the same way. You will have more enjoyment by sharing and connecting than you will just selling, especially if you don't believe you can sell or don't want to be too salesy.

SHARE SMILES & COMPLIMENTS

Want to know the secret to connecting? Making eye contact and smiling. Nowadays it's a breath of fresh air when you actually meet someone's gaze, share a smile or a compliment. If you see someone with a hairstyle you love, or someone wearing a dress in your favorite color or someone holds a door for you, say something! Pay attention to that little voice in your head, the one that quietly says, "what a great pair of shoes," and act upon it. Don't listen to the negative voices in your head that quickly follow up with thoughts like, "she'll think I'm strange for saying something," or, "she's too pretty to speak with me." Listen to your gut; your intuition. Life isn't always about you. In fact, it hardly ever is. And, when you start living for others, that is when you feel most alive. Compliments aren't about you, what you like, or how you are feeling in the moment—they are all about the person you are complimenting. It's about bringing a smile to their face and creating a warm, fuzzy feeling that someone, a random stranger, noticed them and appreciated them in some way.

SHARE BY BEING SOCIAL

As a mompreneur, your business baby needs you to be social. No one has as much belief and passion for your business than you. You can hire people to be the 'front man' but YOU will always be the heart of the business.

Just starting out? You will have to talk and interact with people. Prospects, customers, vendors, retailers and suppliers.

Being social isn't always about speaking eloquently or being intelligent. It's about connecting. When you encounter someone in your market booth, playground, networking event, or other venue, make eye contact and smile! Compliment them (or their kids) and share a comment about something that is relevant and friendly.

The first step in having a conversation is STARTING one! You can't always wait for fate, you've got to take control of your destiny and take the first step. You may feel nervous the first few times (or even seven), but it will get easier the more you do it.

Sitting on a bench with your head buried in a book or phone doesn't help you make connections. Don't get me wrong—a little time to yourself while kids play at the park is bliss, just don't dedicate the whole time to it. Make it a game! Challenge yourself to talk to one person (or three) before you can leave for your next activity. Even if you don't close a sale, you may make a new friend (who could refer you to more friends), or at the very least, have a chance to add another practice conversation under your belt!

At markets or booths, don't just sit and look bored. Would you want to talk to someone who looked uninterested in what was going on around them—perhaps even frowning? Think of it this way, who would you want to connect with? Be that person! Stand up if you can, pocket your cell phone, and smile. If you are bored, inspect your wares like a customer— other people walking by may be intrigued at the sight of you looking through your things.

Being social online may not be as intuitive, but you can do it in your pajamas in the middle of the night! Comment on posts and engage with their content. Don't just like their posts; ask questions or provide value by answering comments and giving advice. Use private messages for topics that may get personal. Commenting on Instagram is even more special than when you do it on Facebook and you are also more likely to get the original poster to view your profile when you tag them in your post.

SHARE BY ASKING QUESTIONS

It's up to you to initiate the conversation. You have a wonderful solution to a problem they may have. They don't know that. They see you and your booth and then glance away. Catch their eye, smile and engage! Open conversations like this: "Beautiful day, isn't it?" "Love your earrings, where'd you get them?" These questions are open-ended and literally asking for a response. Barking out your wares or simply promoting, "buy one, get one!" won't catch a big fish; it may catch one-off purchasers on a budget, but not necessarily your ideal customer.

A conversation is a volley; it's movement is back and forth. You speak, they speak. Repeat. A one-sided conversation is really just a lecture or presentation. The most effective way to ensure the volley continues? Ask questions. Respond to what they have said, then ask a question to keep them talking about themselves. Ask questions which will help you guide or recommend the perfect product. Be sure to engage in the kids of prospective customers. If you're selling accessories, like headbands or bowties at a mom-made market, complement parents on their kid's style and ask the child what their favorite color is, or if they like stripes or dots.

When you have conversations with a new mom at a park, make a connection first by sharing something about yourself and following up with questions. Get to know her as a person. Uncovering her dreams, fears and frustrations provides insight into what products may suit her best. Why share about a product or service that is of no use to her?

Think of it like dating. This could be your meet-cute. It might not lead to a coffee date...but maybe it will. You have to chat, connect and share to see if you will pursue her as a prospect, if she may refer you to one of her friends, or if you will part ways, never to speak again.

☐ *Exercise: Go-to Prospect Questions*
The questions you ask will depend on your business, products or services. If you want to prepare some questions and practice in front of your mirror then I recommend you review your *Persona Profiles* exercise from page 40.

If you haven't done it, go back to Step 4: Plan For Customers and do it. After reviewing the persona profile for your ideal customer, come up with questions that would lead to the information in their profile. Pare those questions down to just three or four that are your go-to's, for when conversations start to slow down while trying to connect with a new person.

Write your questions on a sticky note, in your idea notebook or in a saved note on your phone. Review them when putting on your prospecting hat. Depending on your style, mix it up, using these key questions as a guide, or memorize them. Either way, make sure YOU are shining through. So many times, connections are made not because of what we say, but how we present ourselves and our energy.

SHARE YOUR STORIES

Studies have shown that stories sell products better. I remember reading an article on a social site where a seller created two listings for the same product. One listed just the facts about the item, like size, materials and year made, while the other included a story about how the item had sentimental value. The listing with the story had nearly triple the engagement of the factual listing. The story itself isn't what sells the product better—it's the way the story connects the buyer to the product. It's the connection that leads to the sale.

If you want a deeper connection when sharing about yourself, your product or service, you will need to open up and show depth. Of course, you'll always want to share the factual and measurable information about your products such as colors, features and materials, but it's important to give them a 'life' story too!

Think of it as similar to introducing two of your friends to each other: If you were to say, "Jenn, this is Stephanie. We grew up together," it would sound bland. In fact, later, you may not even remember Stephanie's name.

But what if your friend said, "Jenn, I'd like you to meet a friend of mine. Stephanie is an amazing baker, you should try her watermelon cupcakes! They taste heavenly and always remind me of the summer days we spent at the lake as kids."

While both of these get across the important info, which introduction inspires you to connect with, learn more about and become friends with Stephanie? Your friend didn't 'sell' you on Stephanie—she just shared her personal stories about Stephanie with you, letting her genuine excitement come through.

Now, imagine it wasn't 'Stephanie'; it's one of your products. The same idea applies here. Share about your product's history, how it was designed, why it came about, the inspiration behind it, your hopes for it and the impact it has made in someone else's life. You can also share how it has impacted your life, how things have improved, and why you chose this company or product to sell. As the conversation progresses, share your lifestyle and discuss how the product can fit into everyday life.

If you are selling yourself as a service provider, like a photographer, therapist, accountant or designer, share your experiences, philosophies and passion. Share the story about why you chose this profession or industry, and how you give back by mentoring or providing pro-bono services through non-profit foundations.

SHARE OTHER PRODUCTS

When someone is interested in making a purchase, mention another complementary product that they may not have seen in your offering. Spotlight a product like this: "Most people who buy this also like to get this, too," or "did you see the matching Daddy bow-tie?" It doesn't hurt to share helpful information! Increasing the sale by offering complementary items is called cross-selling, and can prove helpful for your customers.

Upselling is when you offer an enhancement to a product someone already wants. You can do this by offering personalization or promotional offers. For example, if you were selling a child's bowtie, you could offer monogram services; if you wanted to promote a 'BOGO', you could offer a buy-one, get-one at a discount promo. If you're selling services, you could upgrade more hours of work to their package.

Or, look at it another way: upselling is like asking, "Do you want to supersize that?" while cross selling is asking, "Would you like a drink with that?"

SHARE REFERRALS & TESTIMONIALS

Share more than just your business story. Share your customers' stories. Get your existing network to help you share your business. Offer a referral bonus to those who refer new customers or have drawings for customers who write testimonials or product reviews. A testimonial is a customer's story about how your business or product impacted their life. It's a great way to connect a prospect to your product via another customer's experience. Product reviews work the same way, but are used for tangible products while testimonials are good for services.

Another way to share your business is by spotlighting a specific customer in a blog or social media post. These type of customer highlights provide diverse stories for prospects to resonate with, garner more social engagement, and encourage your existing customers to be featured too.

SHARE PROMOTIONS

Continue to come from a sharing space if promotions are something you want to do. Don't spam with, "50% off, buy now!" We get enough of those types of advertisements from big retailers. Direct sales and network marketing are really relationship marketing. When you first start out on your own, the same is true. You'll tap your network first and then look to expand. Ask questions instead of communicating commands. Ask prospects open-ended questions like: "Have you finished your Christmas shopping?", "Have you bought a Valentine's Day gift yet?", "Tired of being unhappy with your health?" Give them some insight into yourself and share stories of how different your life is now. Share how you can improve their lives, and then let them know how lucky they are—because it's perfect timing with your current promotion!

SHARING BY THE NUMBERS

While you don't want to treat each prospect or customer as a number, you should still understand your business's numbers regarding sharing and sales. If you talk to five people and only one person purchases, then for every sale you want, you need to talk to five people. Want four sales this week? Talk to 20 people!

☐ *Exercise: No Goals*

Are you discouraged that you only get one sale for every five people you reach out to? Turn it around. Don't go chasing after the sales or 'Yes' responses. Instead, look at it like you need to find four 'no's or four people who aren't interested in your product. Take a piece of paper and divide it in half lengthwise. Put 'No' as the headline on the first column and 'Yes' on the second. Start talking to people and add tick markers based on their responses. Set goals for your 'No's, not your 'Yes's.

Don't be discouraged if a prospect doesn't buy immediately or even after a few, (or many), follow-ups. Especially in direct sales, it can take time and sharing a lot of information before someone is ready to participate. Be consistent with your approach, foster your connections and be you!

Keep in mind, hearing a 'No' to your products or services does not mean they are rejecting YOU. Your product or service is just not what they feel they need at that time.

When a prospect makes a choice, it's all about them. It's about their life, their situation, their dreams and their fears. Don't make it about YOU. A mompreneur is an amazing woman! You created life—and you can do more in a day on four hours of sleep than half the population of this planet! You are raising and shaping the life other of little humans, so why would you allow someone's rejection for your candles, business opportunity or photography packages to make a dent on your beautiful soul? You are meant to do ridiculously amazing things with your life, and being a mom is proof that you are already doing so! You made another human and now you are birthing a business into this world! Sure, it can feel scary at times. Remember the first day, how gingerly you held your child? How carefully you were to do it 'right?' Even if you had a village of support around you, you still had to figure out what would be best for you and your baby. Eventually, it was no longer so scary. Things got better as you learned your baby and experienced things together as a family. And, as with growth of all things, new challenges arose for you to work through. Even now, there are times you feel like a bad mom and others where you feel like a super mom. That's motherhood—and it's also the same for being an entrepreneur. It can feel scary at times, and you may be unsure of the right way to do things. During those times, reflect and do what you did as a new mom. Ask for advice, research and then try a few things to see what works best. You'll eventually get through that situation or phase and have a new adventure waiting for you to experience. And, just like motherhood, you'll end up with an amazing reward—your business baby, that takes on a life and personality of its own. Best of all, you get to be the proud momma who made it all happen!

SHARING THROUGH FUNNELS

When it comes to sharing and selling, part of knowing your business numbers is understanding your conversion funnel. A quick search on Google or Facebook will provide you a plethora of information about funnels including freebies and webinars on how to implement them and strategies to grow them. Just the term 'sales funnel' can feel daunting when you are first starting out, but understanding the how and why of something makes it less scary. A funnel is just the path it takes a for a prospect to achieve a goal, such as make a purchase, join your mailing list or complete a lead form. Along the way, some prospects don't proceed while others move on to the next step, thus creating a funnel-like behavior. There are a lot prospects in the beginning, but closer to the end of the purchasing process, there are less. Creating a diagram can help you visualize where you can improve the flow and give you a better idea on how to hit your goals.

☐ *Exercise: Get To Know Your Conversion Rates*

Get a piece of paper and draw a funnel (or upside down triangle with the bottom open). At the top of your funnel is everyone who enters your process; at the bottom are those who completed all the steps to get to your goal. You can better understand the actions you need to take to hit your goals by generating a conversion rate for each funnel step. A **conversation rate** is the percentage of people that move on, or convert, from one step to the next. You can use the formula **# Completed / # Started**. For instance, if 100 people visit your web site and 5 join your mailing list, then your mailing list conversion rate is 5 ÷ 100 = 5%.

Let's look at a candlemaker's sales funnel. While the specific steps may be different for your funnel, product and business, the general idea and math will still apply.

The start of this funnel is a product webpage about a red candle. In one month, it was viewed 100 times and added to a cart 15 times. The first step of the funnel is the person's action of viewing the product page; the next step is adding it to the cart. The conversation rate is found by taking the next step number divided by the first step. In this example, we divide 15 product additions to the cart by 100 views (15 ÷ 100). This gives us the red candle's **add to cart conversion rate** of 15%.

Of those 15 candles added to a cart, only three were actually purchased. So, to figure out the red candle's **cart purchase conversion rate,** we now divide 3 purchases by 15 adds to the cart (3 ÷ 15). This tells us that the cart purchase conversion rate for the red candle is 20%.

Note: You could also find this funnel's **overall purchase conversion rate**, by dividing 3 purchases by 100 product page views. This gives you a 3% conversion rate.

Let's take those conversion rates and use them to find what our **page views goals** should be, if we want to sell $100 worth of red candles each month. In this example, the candlemaker is currently selling 3 candles each for $10, a month for total of $30. If they want to sell $100 worth v of red candles each month, they will need to sell 10 candles. So, how many people need to view the product page to make the candlemaker's sales goal?

To figure this out, take the product quantity goal of 10, and divide it by your overall funnel conversion rate of 3% in decimal form (3 ÷ 100 = 0.03). So, 10 divided by .03 equals 333.33 red candle product page views needed to sell the goal of 10 candles. It's best to always round up from a decimal, so 334 would be your product page view goal.

Using these formulas keeps you from stressing about how to sell more product. This type of math analysis lets you know exactly how many people you need to share it with, to hit your sales goal!

SHARING IN THE FOLLOW UP, TOO

Sorry, but the process doesn't end when you've make the sale. You've gone to great lengths to connect and educate people about you, your business and your product, so why not encourage future purchases by continuing to connect and share with them? After someone completes a purchase, use the thank you page or their online receipt to invite them to follow you on Facebook or join your email list to learn about new products, promotions and upcoming events. Draft your email receipts carefully. Don't just provide the bare minimum of their order details. Instead, include links to your social networks, info on how to opt-in for your newsletter and offer a coupon for their next purchase.

If you're selling in-store or at a market, you can update your printed receipts or slip a postcard into their bag with a promo and information on ways they can connect with your business. If you are shipping a product, include a postcard or even a handwritten thank you card. A note like that helps the customer feel special and less like a transaction.

Important! Never make a connection with a prospect and forget about them! Use social media to follow up with your fans and followers in a general way, and use your mailing list to follow up with your customers directly. Where possible, follow up with customers in a personal way—try sending a short, personalized text via direct message or email. At an event, when you see them again, start another conversation to deepen the connection. Try to use their name to show them that you remember them. Knowing and using someone's name is a great way to make a connection beyond the transaction at-hand. If you are nervous about talking to prospects, practice speaking with others when you are out in public. Nearly every shop employee, waitress or clerk wears a name tag—the info is there for a reason, so use it! When they ask you, "Can I help you?", respond with, "Yes, (name on nametag), I am looking for..." When checking out or leaving the store say, "Thank you, (name on nametag)." It only takes a brief moment to read their name tag and it can make a difference in their day (and the level of service they provide you, too).

SHARING SCHEDULE

Set aside time, either daily or every few days, to connect with your customers.

First, reach out to three new potential prospects (people who you haven't yet reached out to about your product or services). Strike up a conversation—you could remind them about how you initially met, or simply share how much you love their recent Facebook post. Continue with the flow of the conversation, weaving in your excitement in your new business venture. Share some info about your products in a casual way and ask if they know of anyone who may be interested in it. Don't start off asking for their interest in it; ask for referrals first. If they are interested, you'll get a 'Yes, me!' or a comment like, "I might be, tell me more," kind of response. It's easier to ask someone for help with referrals than it is to ask for a sale.

SHARE RESPONSIBILY

Following up and building connections does not include sending out a mass email to all of your contacts at one time. This is about connecting; starting and engaging in conversation. Demonstrating how you will treat them as a customer and not just as a number. It also reduces the flow of responses to something you can manage. Imagine what would happen if you got your list of 100 or more contacts all to respond! It would be a fun problem to have, but managing 10 conversations can get complicated, let alone 100! If you start conversations with three or five people a day you can respond more comfortably. Once you get the hang of things, you can increase the amount of people you contact or decrease that number based on your time and business needs.

After this, follow up with 3-5 prospects you've already initiated a conversation with. They could be someone who reached out with a question or filled out a lead form on your website. Continue an engagement philosophy but remember to ask for the sale! A few ways you can ask for their approval so you can move to the next phase in your process include: "Are you ready to move forward today?" "When would you want to start?" or, "What other concerns may I alleviate for you, before you are willing to make a purchase?"

Lastly, show some love to a few of your existing customers. Send a handwritten thank you note, or pick up the phone and give them a call to check in and say hello—without any intention of selling them something.

Send a Facebook message or text telling them you are thinking about them and hope they have a wonderful day. Brighten their day by reminding them how important they are to you—that they are more than just a number or a sale. Be sure you mix up the order and frequency when you reach out to your existing customers. Spread the love to all of your customers, not just your favorites or repeat customers. Reaching out to one-time purchasers may lead them to be inspired to become a repeat customer.

STEP 8: ORGANIZE

I've come to realize that I am more productive when I have a full to-do list with fully scheduled days for the simple fact that those are filled with 'have-tos'. Meetings have to happen, soccer practice, and holiday parties. And, of course, the dishes and laundry too.

The reason moms are great multi-taskers isn't because we were born this way. Science has proven that multitasking is impossible. Our brains don't allow us to do complex processes at the exact same time. Most of what people consider 'multitasking' is the act of quickly switching from one task to another. So, the way to become a good multitasker is to increase your ability to pick up an activity or process. Because of this, raising kids (small humans whose very survival depends on us) has conditioned us to move from task to task as efficiently as possible. As a mompreneur, you'll need to take it to the next level—you need to look at your to-do lists and say bring it on!

Some ways to help you accomplish better success with multi-tasking is to mentally separate from one task to another by changing your state of mind with other physical sensations. Signal your mind that it's time to work with a ritual, like listening to a specific music playlist, lighting aromatherapy candles or doing some yoga. If you are in a really stubborn mindset and can't seem to get focused on work, try a change of environment. Take a walk, do a load of laundry or take a shower. I find these transitions highly effective, especially when switching from a logical task to a creative task or when talking to a prospect after dealing with a frustrating client.

ORGANIZE YOUR SPACE

A separate and organized workspace (or dedicated area removed from other tasks and activities) keeps it free from tangible clutter as well as mental clutter. (Have you ever sat down to write a thank you note and got distracted with a bill or grocery list?) Keep distractions at bay by cueing your brain and body that your designated space is an area for working.

If you can't have a dedicated, separate area, it's even more important that it be organized and clear of clutter. If it is a shared space, ensure each task your area has to accommodate has clearly defined storage areas such as: drawers, files, shelves, baskets, etc. If you know exactly where everything is, you don't have to waste time hunting for your stapler or riffling through papers to find your notes on a new contract.

Remember, you are choosing to work in this area. Show gratitude toward the space and your efforts by making it comfortable to you. Using a chair you hate or a desk with water rings that always make you scowl is not going to be productive for you. Use a different chair. Repaint the desk or finally do one of those Pinterest hacks you've been telling yourself you'd eventually accomplish. Spending time on these improvements now, will make your future work time more pleasant and productive.

Creating a business from scratch can be lovely. You are gestating ideas, researching, contemplating and spending a lot of time examining the thoughts in your mind. It's important to add an element of beauty or inspiration to your work area, which will improve your mood and environment. A flower, framed motivational quote, geode or figurine can be your visual cue to focus on business. If the element brings you a smile, reminds you of your motivation, adds a bit of sparkle or connects you with your 'spirit animal', then by all means, embrace it! Just don't go so overboard that your work space is full of inspiration, but without enough room for you to actually work. My elements catch my attention while I revel in thought and bring me a spark of joy. They remind me of my purpose and why I am strive to achieve my dreams and goals.

ORGANIZE YOUR SCHEDULE

Shifting gears to more practical business matters…

If you haven't already done so, please complete the *Open For Business* exercise on page 33 from Step 3: Prioritize Your Calendar to determine your standard business hours.

After you've determined your business hours, you need to create a business schedule using a calendar or planner. There are SO many different planners, systems and apps for you to choose from, so use whatever method works best for you. I split my time between phone and laptop, so I found a solution that easily syncs between my devices and can be shared with others (e.g. my husband, family, business partners, etc.) I prefer to use Google Calendar as it allows multiple, sharable and color-coded calendars along with advanced recurrence features. Also, most third party apps and services integrate well with it. My favorite is the iOS Calendars+ app, as it syncs with all of my Google Calendars, keeps their color coding and has a great 'day view', that is nearly identical to the Google Calendar web interface.

⬚ *Exercise: Time Blocking*

With your calendar at-hand, start blocking or reserving time within your business hours for specific tasks. When do you plan to call on customers, market, send out invoices or create your product? Of course, flexibility is key; you will probably need to move things around as you schedule calls and take care of priority projects. Having a plan guides your day. It provides you with the mental freedom to focus on what you have scheduled—and not what is scheduled for later.

Scheduling a power hour in the morning empowers you to start your day with dedication to building your dreams. Block out the time to get in the zone and focus on doing work. It's even more productive when you can dedicate that time to income-producing activities, like marketing, following up with prospects, writing proposals, sending out invoices, enrolling a new business builder, posting products on your site, etc.

Keep in mind, not every hour you work will be billable. You have to schedule dedicated time for business housekeeping. You will need time to respond to emails, conduct market research, strategize, etc. Try to dedicate at least 30 minutes a day, (ideally, 30 minutes in the morning and evening,) for following up with prospects and customers via email or social media. Blocking time for these activities keeps you from checking in at every moment and distracting you from money-making activities. It's best to schedule time for longer, less frequent business housekeeping tasks like monthly marketing planning or invoicing.

While blocking out your schedule, ensure enough time to accomplish the tasks. Overestimate. While a task may only require 10 minutes, it may actually take 30 if kids are around! In addition, don't block out 100% of your time with tasks. Leave some gaps to schedule things that may come up during the day or room to reschedule if something else takes longer than expected.

If necessary, be sure to plan for transit time and traffic. Your day will feel so much better when you plan ahead, arrive early and discover you have a few extra moments to handle business! You'll be able to jot down ideas in your notebook and respond to emails instead of arriving late and feel rushed and stressed. Plan for the chaos and be grateful for the extra time.

Blocking family time like dinners, homework help and fun time with kids is important too. Remember, 'Mom' comes first in the word, Mompreneur. See where you can maximize your time—sports practice may be a great time for you to take calls or respond to prospects on social networks. While being present with your kids is important, your business requires quality time too. Create moments that are family-only or business-only and realize that there are times your attention must be shared.

Scheduling time for yourself each day empowers you to focus on you and not just all of your to-dos. Create a daily practice of the things that fill up your body, mind and soul. Try something like a gratitude journal, devotional or create a daily practice that can include things like yoga, affirmations, and intention setting.

ORGANIZE YOUR TASKS

Implement a task-tracking system for your business. (Even better, find one you can use for managing your mom life too!)

I use the iOS app called "GoTasks", to track my tasks. (I love it because it links directly into my Google account.) It is flexible and allows me to have multiple lists or categories that I can color-code. I can either view all of my tasks, or just tasks on a specific list. Each task can contain additional notes, be set to repeat for a specific time, have reminders and/or deadlines. I use lists for myself, the household chores, groceries, and each of my businesses.

Whether you use apps, digital planning tools, a notebook or sticky notes, the important part is that you USE something! Make sure the system you use is one that you feel confident in keeping up with. If you leave pieces of papers all over the house and spend time rummaging around for your to-do list, that's not going to be helpful in keeping you organized and efficient for a successful business.

STEP 9: SUPPORT

Like a breastfeeding momma, your business baby solely relies on you for nourishment. Therefore; it's up to you to provide for yourself, in order to provide for it. Finding support is imperative. Just like parenting, it can be done on your own, but the bigger your support team, the easier things seem. Each mom and each business is different, so try a few of these suggestions and see which work best for you, your business, and your family.

SUPPORT YOURSELF

It's important to give yourself what you need. Self-care and self-love support you to feel better about yourself.

> *"When you feel good, you do good!"*
>
> *Johnette Gambrell*

Self-care means taking care of yourself the way you take care of the rest of the family. Showering, dressing appropriately, spending time outside, moving your body, and not being in front of a screen all day are self-love requirements. They're all the things you nag your kids about!

You are the most important asset of your business. Just like a child, it needs you for its very survival. At its early stages, without you, or another designated caregiver, it will cease to exist. So, to be able to give your business baby the best you can, you need to ensure you are taking care of yourself, too. I recommend putting yourself first, but depending on your current stage of motherhood, that might not be possible. Do what you can. Be gentle with yourself. When you feel your energy drying up, pause and attend to yourself. Stop pushing through. If you don't take care of yourself, things will only get harder—you will feel more frustration and may even begin to feel resentment toward your business, kids or yourself. Then, the guilt could set in and make you feel even worse. Stop the cycle by recognizing and addressing your own needs.

> ## *"You cannot serve from an empty vessel."*
> *Eleanor Brown*

As in all action, you can choose the size of step you take to care for yourself. Maybe it's turning on the TV or tablet for the kids so you can have a hot shower in peace. Or, heading to the park, sitting back and enjoying an indulgent coffee or smoothie. Better yet, maybe it's treating your body to stress-reducing exercise, a pedicure or massage! Self-love is taking a nap, sleeping in, or connecting with another passion that's separate from your business. Cook! Garden, paint or read a magazine or book; connect with your higher power through prayer or meditation. You are the sum of your body, mind and soul. When one or more of these areas become depleted, your mood and productivity will be impacted.

Get Away

Some time off and way from your work space provides separation from its stresses and thoughts. So, get out of the house or away from your office during times of stress and frustration. A daily walk outdoors can switch up your energy and mood. If you work from home, it can be even harder to disconnect, so take a vacation—even if it's a half-day break to your favorite beach, park, spa, etc. Disconnect from your work, switch scenery, thought patterns, and recharge.

The longer you skip this time away physically and mentally, the longer you'll need to recharge when you do get around to taking a traditional vacation. (And, let's be honest: as a mom, family vacations are not restful experiences. Traveling with family carries the extra burden of new environments, adjusted schedules and the strange combination of overtired and hyper kids.) That's not much of a break for your mental state!

Be Flexible and Open

Being flexible is a huge support to your business and family as a mompreneur. Yes, it's important to plan your work and work your plan, but be open to adjustments. A rigid attitude can lead to unnecessary stress for you and your family when things come up, which they usually do. Be flexible with your tactics and strategies. Try new things. If they don't work, don't give up, tweak something. Twist, bend and move until you find what works for you. Don't set rules but guidelines, and create a plan for what you want to do if things do go off track or need to be adjusted.

Let Go of Perfection

As moms, we always take on more than we should. If it's got to get done, we think it's easier for us to do it, and then we know it will get done right. But, do things really need to get done 'right'? Is it really a concern of 'right' vs. "'wrong'? Or, is it more about 'your way' vs. 'another way'? I'm talking about more than just concerns over how the dishwasher is loaded. Delegating is a hard thing to learn for all of the Super Moms out there (myself included!), but a clean spoon is still a clean spoon, no matter which way it was loaded into the dishwasher!

"Done is better than perfect."

Sheryl Sandberg

Why put the stress of perfection on yourself? Or, on others who are doing what they can to support you like your family, partner or assistant? As a mom, do you demand perfection from your child? Do you applaud them for trying, for their effort? Why not give yourself the same kind of acknowledgement as a business owner?

"Perfection is a myth.
There is so much more beauty in imperfection."

Cynthia Morehouse, CynthiaMorehouse.etsy.com

Why strive for perfection? Why strive to be what someone else tells you that you need to be? Find your flaws, cracks and acknowledge them for what makes you truly beautiful, unique and interesting.

Find Your Happy

Give yourself the tools to succeed, the mindset to find happiness, and the time to accomplish what you've set out to do. If you aren't happy, why are you doing it? If it doesn't move you forward, why do you proceed?

Connecting with your joy, passion, bliss and happiness supports you to get through complicated situations, holiday rush and nights of projectile kid vomit! Continually check in with your joy; be flexible and make changes to your schedule, tasks, and tactics, to keep you enjoying life and the entrepreneurial journey you are on.

Be okay if things change. Did you start out as a stay-at-home mom and you're now thinking of working from home? Have you discovered that you want or need to go back into a corporate position as a working mom? Do what is right for you and your family. First, choose love and happiness.

Then, decide what to choose for your profession. Remember, life isn't black and white. You can be a mompreneur and still work a 9-5 job. You can have it all, just maybe not all at the same time. The more on your plate, the fuller your schedule, so it make take longer for you to reach your goals. Just keep taking steps forward!

Don't Compare Yourself to Others

Compare your products, pricing and brand for market research to see where there are opportunities to make tweaks to improve your business success. Don't compare your journey with someone else. Don't compare your worth, your value or aptitude for success based on someone else. Doing so opens the door for a lot of negative thoughts, creates self-doubt and diminishes your drive to act. There are plenty of people in the world who will tell you that you can't, that you aren't enough. Don't let your own voice join them.

Be your own cheerleader. Believe in yourself despite what they say. Hell, believe in yourself despite what you think or what the voices in your head say! Those voices are just shadows or memories of what other people have said to you as you grew up. Don't let their version of your past history stop you from writing your own happy ending.

Fuel your body

The old adage is true, you are what you eat. If you eat garbage don't be surprised if you feel like garbage! Eating well fuels your body for all the crazy things you have to do as a Mom and business owner.

First, don't live on coffee—most coffee is too acidic for our bodies and can do more harm long-term than the morning (or afternoon) pick-me-up, you feel you need right now. Try to cut back or find an alternative like green tea.

Replace packaged and processed snacks with fresh snacks like veggies or fruit. Opt for organics if you can. The better the ingredients that go into a recipe–the better the dish. It's the same for your body!

Eat breakfast and I don't mean grabbing a donut at Starbucks or a fast food egg sandwich. After hours of sleep, your body needs fuel to get you through your busy morning. Give it the good stuff! Start with a protein-rich meal to keep you full and energized—try some eggs and spinach, oatmeal with nuts and cranberries, or a meal replacement shake with a big dose of the nutrients you need to start your morning right.

Did you know that your body can only create energy or create fat? It can't do both at the same time! Observe how you feel after eating different things. Do you feel energized or lethargic? Which way would you prefer to feel? Lethargic mompreneurs have to take naps to get through the day. Energized mompreneurs power through income-producing activities.

If you won't do it for yourself, do it for your business!

Get Your Sleep

Stop sacrificing sleep. Sleep is extremely necessary for our health and well-being. Staying up until 4 a.m. may help you finish your deadline, but it eats into the energy resources for your next day, then the next, until you crash or get sick, all the while hating how you feel, and maybe even getting short-tempered with your kids, husband or even customers! Not good. Get some sleep.

While we sleep, our brains have a chance to detox from any emotional build up and save any memories from our experiences of the day. If you have had a stressful day, give yourself some extra shut-eye. Opt to let something else slide so you can take care of yourself. Sleep also affects how short term memory becomes long term memory, so getting more sleep can improve your mental clarity and recall. Sleep even assists in weight loss! Do you get the point yet? Sleep!

Allow enough time in your schedule for 6-8 hours. Don't binge watch five TV episodes and then head to bed. Set limits. Set guidelines with yourself on the number of episodes you will watch or how many chapters you'll read before turning out the lights. And stick to those limits.

If you are sleep training a newborn or a toddler who constantly gets up at night, be gentle with yourself. Listen to your body when it needs more sleep. Take a power nap during the day and enjoy some sleep cuddles with your little one. Turn off the alarm and snooze! The to-do list can wait. Just don't make it a habit—you don't want to sleepwalk through life, but don't be a mombie either!

SUPPORTIVE WORDS

We can affect the way we think and feel about situations by the use of our words and reactions. As moms, it's not just our own self-talk we should be aware of, but the words we say out loud that little ears can hear as well.

Be careful of using the words, 'have to'. There is little in life we literally 'have to' do (although breathing and keeping the kids alive do come to mind). Most everything falls into a category of things you choose to do (that you may not like doing) in anticipation of a specific outcome. For example, "I have to go to work," really means that you are choosing to go to work in order to get paid money to support your family. "I have to do the dishes" really means that you are choosing to do the dishes so that your house does not smell and the dishes are clean for the next meal. At first, it may feel forced to change 'have to' statements to 'choose to'. You can also use, "I get to" as an alternative, which also helps you come from a place of gratitude. Personally, I just can't get behind the statement, "I get to do the dishes!" Instead, I like to use the phrase, "It's time to." While saying, "I choose to," (as in, "I choose to go to work") or, "I get to," may be understood by an adult, "It's time to," is easier to explain to a toddler. It also demonstrates the importance of following a schedule and focusing on a specific task within a specific timeframe. This is a good practice for both mompreneurs and developing kids. And, it makes the statement, "it's time to do the dishes" much easier to say than, "I get to do the dishes."

The word 'need' is similar to the phrase 'have to'. Use 'commit to' instead. "I need to do the laundry today," turns into, "I commit to doing the laundry today." Or, "I need to follow up with three prospects," turns into "I commit to follow up with three prospects."

Never use the word, 'can't'! You have the ability within you to do ANYTHING you set your mind to. Come from a place of choice and use the word, 'won't', instead. That way, you aren't limiting your abilities— you are simply choosing to do what you are interested in now.

Be conscious of how you use the phrase 'I am'. Keep things positive and even aspirational like, "I am a successful mompreneur," or, "I make connections easily and authentically." Be wary of using it when describing experiences. "I am sick" and "I am tired" are not things you ARE, they are things you are experiencing or feeling, so define them as such: "I am feeling sick," or, "I am feeling tired."

SUPPORTIVE SPOUSE

Having your husband or partner's support of your endeavor can make the difference between a happy family and not, let alone a successful business. If they are automatically supportive and encouraging, sit down together and share your ideas, goals and plans. Specifically discuss how family duties may need to be adjusted. The sharing of responsibilities like chores, school drop-offs, sports, parties, cleaning, cooking and shopping will free you up from feeling guilty about not getting it all done. (It may also teach your partner and kids that dishes don't magically clean themselves!)

If your spouse is less than supportive, dedicate some time, like a date night or an evening stroll for discussing things. Ask questions to understand their reservations about your ideas. Share how important their support is to you. Share your motivation and your goals and then ask for their support. Ask them to give you a chance to at least try for success. Set a time frame, like three or six months, and ask them what goals would help them see this trial as a success. Get their buy-in, that they will be supportive of your endeavor after you have met those goals. Request their full support for the duration of the trial so that you will be set up for success. Discuss what will happen if the goal doesn't get met for your trial. Will you be asked to quit? Will you be able to review and adjust? What happens if you exceed the goal, or almost achieve it? Continue to ask questions to get a better understanding of their concerns. Listen. Take notes. Don't try to convince them that their views are wrong. After listening to their concerns, work to educate them on everything you have learned.

Use language that is affirmative, not defensive. Where appropriate, you can respond to their statements with things like, "That's a valid point." Or, "I was concerned by that too," or "I researched and discovered…" And, if you don't have an answer to a question right away, you could say, "I hadn't thought of it like that. I'd like time to research and get back to you."

It's important to understand if there are non-business concerns so that you can set appropriate expectations, like how much time you'll spend with the kids, when dinner will be on the table and how household chores will be divided up. Set expectations for both of you. This may be your dream to build a business, but raising a family is a team sport. Make sure all players know the game plan.

SUPPORTIVE KIDS

If your kids are old enough to ask questions, then start telling them about the things you are doing for your business. Share your excitement; share your dreams. Let them feel your energy and passion. Show them that you are scared too, but are doing it anyway. Being an example of hard work, ingenuity, independence and entrepreneurism will leave a much bigger impact on your children than just talking about these ideals.

With toddlers and preschoolers, you can have them help carry and move things from one pile to another, or match items. I like to make a game of fulfilling my Etsy orders by asking my three-year-old to find me bags of beads in specific colors. Of course, it takes longer than if I just did it myself, but my son is always excited to 'help' mommy with the orders. Plus, he gets to learn the difference in color between teal and mint. (Something my husband still doesn't know!)

Match the level involvement, types of tasks and time spent helping, with your child's age and competency. Make games of it to make it fun for them and you. Competitions, like who can stuff the most envelopes or stamp their pile the fastest, make things fun—just keep an eye out for the quality too.

NOT-SO SUPPORTIVE PEOPLE

Do you have naysayers in your immediate circle of family and friends? Those you just KNOW will say things like, "You will fail", "No one will ever buy that", or "MLMs are all schemes!"?

You have two choices with how to deal with them: you can listen to them—or not.

It's your choice to believe what they say or believe in yourself. If you don't want to hear it from them, reach out and tell them straight up: "I'm committing to doing this. I would love your support and encouragement, but if you aren't able to, please at least support me by refraining to tell me how I'm doing it wrong or how I will fail." You may be surprised how starting a conversation like this opens up a channel for you to start sharing how their words and actions have affected you previously.

SUPPORT GROUPS

The Internet has enabled niche groups to find each other and grow. If you can think it up, there is a Facebook group, Meet-up or forum for it.

Search for local or national mom blogs or associations. They can help you connect with other moms in your area and many have subgroups and interests. Search online groups or meet-up events to find other like-minded entrepreneurs. You may find a mompreneur group or a group specific to your product. Be open-minded and try it out. Interact with the members. Ask for advice, answer questions, share your story. Share with members but do not 'sell'. These support groups are to help you grow, see the competition or just vent with others in the same situation. It's a totally different goal than the groups you'd join to find your ideal customers. If a member of the group reaches out to you privately, showing interest in your business, then treat them as a prospect.

SUPPORTIVE HELP

There are only so many hours in the day. If your schedule is getting too full, think about hiring help. You can have a mommy's helper or nanny to help out with the kids or a virtual assistant to help with some of the business tasks. Hire a cleaning crew and use grocery delivery services (some offer free delivery based on your purchase). Delegate. There is only one of you in this world and your mission in life isn't doing dishes.

Hire professionals to help with things you don't know how to do. Sure, you can totally learn to do them yourself, but it will take longer and be a bumpier road. Invest in your business, but be smart about it. Just because you can pay $10,000, on your website doesn't mean you'll see $10,000, worth of added value to your business. Shop around, be clear about what your expectations are and remember to refer to your business and family budget. Calculate how much time you will be able to put back into your business and how much revenue it will bring in. Make sure your investments make financial sense.

In addition, look to hiring a coach or consultant to keep you on track, motivated and growing. You may be able to find a friend who is willing to be an accountability partner or business mentor—which is awesome! Keep in mind, however; that they may not be as invested with their time and availability as a paid coach.

There are many coaches for different niches…real estate, entrepreneurial, success/life coaches and business consultants. Google and Facebook groups are a great place to start your search for them. You'd be surprised how you can find a perfect match, like a jewelry-maker momma, Etsy guru or outdoor photography stylist and coach. Take advantage of any free offers they have (usually they offer a freebie to join their mailing list). See how they interact on social media, and if they have a free introductory call to test the waters before scheduling sessions. Coaches don't have a magic potion that will make you successful overnight, but they can share experiences, exercises and tools to get you there faster than you would on your own. They are also a great resource for talking through ideas, networking with other like-minded people or connecting with other professional resources, as well as for working on your personal development.

SUPPORTIVE SYSTEMS

Document your processes and systems. When you write down all the steps you do to complete a task, such as launching a product, then you can see the full picture as well as the details. You can also see where you can delegate to an assistant or outsource to a professional.

This list of tasks can then easily turn into a checklist. Add a column and assign dates and voila—it's now a schedule! When using this as a schedule, add a column for how long each task should take—use either timing, such as 15-minute increments or dates. If you want the product to launch on the 15th of the month, work backwards based on the time-to-complete column of your schedule to see when you need to start each step and when each step needs to be completed. If you are working with multiple people, add a column to identify those responsible for completing each task. Now you have a project plan!

It can be most useful to have a 'high level' view of a project plan or schedule with the main tasks and dates, and then break down those tasks further in separate pages. If you have a partner, employees, work with a virtual assistant or have hired a professional designer or marketer, this plan can be shared to train them and ensure each step is accounted for.

This process can be done for any group of tasks in your business: invoicing, new client onboarding, launching a product, going to a convention or market show, launching a promotion, publishing a blog article, etc. There are some apps, like 17Hats and CoMindWork that can help document, schedule and remind you of these project plans and deadlines. If you don't know how long a task should take, guesstimate higher then you'd think and the next time you do it, time yourself.

SUPPORT FOR YOUR EDUCATION

Set aside time in your schedule to expand your horizons. It's up to you to know how much you need to learn and how much to invest. Even if you think you are on top of your game, there are always new levels of mastery to attain.

Listen to podcasts in the car or social media strategy webinars instead of binge-watching Netflix! Google thought-leaders or coaches and follow their social media accounts. Read their blogs and sign up for their free challenges and resources. If you want to delve deeper, buy their products. Keep in mind that buying a tool doesn't improve your business—it's using the tool or acting on what they are teaching or sharing that makes it happen. It won't matter if you sign up for all of the freebies that you can find, or spend thousands on eCourses, seminars or coaching. If you don't read their materials, watch their videos, do their exercises or and take action, you and your business won't grow. Think of it like a treehouse: you can download all the plans you want or invest in a prefab kit, but at some point you'll need to pick up the hammer and get building.

I've had clients who watch webinars, take action and grow. Others who have invested thousands in programs but never got around to using them. There isn't a wrong way to take action—as long as you are taking action, you are learning! If you aren't taking action, then you're stockpiling opportunity.

Depending on your business and personal experiences, you may need more formal education, specialized training or certification. While it may seem like work, keep in mind that with each minute of reading, learning or taking a test you are expanding your knowledge. You are growing and becoming more than you were the day before.

By the way, you don't only have to educate yourself in business-specific areas. Maybe you've always wanted to try a barre class or tango dancing lessons? If doing so helps you grow personally, then do it! Besides, you never know who you may meet or in what way you may be inspired because of your new experiences.

STEP 10: OPTIMIZE

You've come so far! You've dreamed and planned, scheduled and shared and even earned your first dollar!

Keep it up! But don't get stagnate. Your business baby is always evolving and what worked last year or last week may not work this week. Just like when your toddler who loved peas, suddenly wouldn't touch anything green!

To continue growing your business and achieving whatever success looks like to you, you need to review how things are going and try new things to optimize your results.

Take the temperature of your business on a regular basis. Depending on your business, that might be weekly, monthly or quarterly. This temperature check-in should be mainly for your business, with you reporting numbers and tracking progress to your goals. It's also a good time to check in with yourself as a mompreneur. How is your motivation? How are things working with your family?

Take a look back for the last period and make three lists: what worked, what didn't and what ideas you have for improvements. In the corporate world, this exercise is called a **post-mortem** or **retrospective.**

For each win—awesome! Way to go Momma! You are doing it!

For each thing that didn't work, think back to what went wrong. Follow the chain of activities back until you can find what instigated the problem. Once you know the real cause, think of a way to either fix it now or find a way to reduce the chance of it happening again. This is called **root cause analysis**. For a photographer, let's say you were a week late delivering photos to a customer. You would ask yourself 'why'. Then you would follow up with, 'Because,' until you ran out of reasons for why something happened.

Example: Photos were delivered over a week late.
- Why? Because you didn't get enough time to edit.
- Why? Because of your child's soccer tournament over the weekend.
- Why? Because your client did not send final selections on time.
- Why? Because I didn't communicate the need for them to select photos by a specific date.
- Why? Because I forgot.

Sometimes you will find something you need to tweak in your process or workflow and sometimes it's completely out of your hands. Either way, you can be more aware of the warning signs so that next time it happens, you can tell the customer of a possible delay or issue.

OPTIMIZE YOUR NUMBERS

As a small business, there is a lot you can get away without knowing, yet if you want to have a successful business, you're going to need to educate yourself about business, or hire someone you trust, who knows their stuff.

Here are some business terms for different numbers that will help you understand the health of your business better, as well as some ideas for how you can improve them.

Revenue or Gross Sales

These are your business's total revenue including orders, invoices, commissions and every other amount of money the company has brought in. This is usually the number that companies reference when they say they are multimillion dollar companies. They may have sold a million dollars of soap or had a $10,000 month, but that does not mean they made that much in profits.

To increase your revenue, you need to increase the sharing and marketing of your products and services. Be diligent in following up with prospects and existing customers.

Expenses

These are the things your company spends money on, including bills, materials, wages, office supplies, equipment, software, professional services, items, online marketing, hosting, rent, etc.

To reduce your expenses, you'll want to look at saving money, even when you spend it. Search for coupons, look for wholesale pricing and make sure you are spending your marketing dollars in a smart way.

Net or Net Profit

Your business's net profit is total revenue minus expenses.

Profit = Revenue - Expenses

To increase your profit, you can increase your revenue, reduce your expenses, or both!

You always want your revenue to be more than your expenses, otherwise you won't have a profit and will be operating at a loss. This means your company isn't making money for you, it's taking money from you. This may be the case in your first month or six, depending on your business. In the start-up world, they prefer to use the term pre-revenue to imply they are starting out and have not yet made a profit.

Average Order Size or Average Order Amount

The average order size or average order amount is used to see if you are earning more money or selling more per order from one period to the next.

In a specific period, like a month or year, count the number of orders and also calculate the total sum of those order amounts.

Average Order Size = Value of Order ÷ Number of Orders

To increase average order amount, look to promotions with a target value. For instance, if your average order amount is $25, then offer free shipping with orders over $50.

Sometimes average order size describes the number of items in an order instead of its amount. In that case, divide the count of all items in the period by the number of orders. To increase the average order quantity, look to use 'two for' deals.

Cost Per Acquisition

How much does it cost for you to gain a new customer? Look at your marketing spend for social ads, your time at events or markets as well as your expenses like print items and booth fees.

You can choose to calculate cost per acquisition based on a specific period or a single event like an online sale or craft market. Take the total cost for your selected period and divide it by the number of new customers you landed. Depending on your business, that may mean the number of new email subscribers or actual purchasers.

This is important with talking to possible business partners. If it costs you $10 per new customer and they want 30 new customers per month, you know you will need to budget $300/month for marketing.

It is also important to ensure you aren't losing money with your marketing. If it costs $10 to get a customer and the average order amount is $30, that seems like a win! However; if your costs on that $30 order are $25 then you made no profit and in fact, lost $5. If that is the case, try promotions to increase the initial order size or incentives for follow-up purchases. It's okay to not break even on the first order. If your customer averages three orders with a lifetime revenue of $500, then a $10 investment is worth it!

Lifetime Customer Orders & Value

Calculate **Average Orders by Customer** by taking the total orders you have, and dividing them by the total customers. To get your **Average Lifetime Customer Value**, divide the sum of all of your orders by the total customers.

Example: Let's say you have five orders this month purchased by three clients:

- Client A placed an order for $70
- Client B placed an order for $50
- Client B placed an order for $10
- Client C placed an order once for $10
- Client A placed an order for $10

Your Average Orders by Customer would be $50 ($150 ÷ 3) and your Average Monthly Customer Value would also be $50 (Client A $80, Client B $60, Client C $10 or $150 ÷ 3). Here is where the numbers don't always tell the truth:

Averages don't give an accurate depiction of your true business expectation, so take a look at your median values as well. An average is one amount divided by another. A mean is based on a sorted list of values and the middle of the list is selected as the value. Looking at the example, your average customer value would be $50 but your mean customer value for the month would be $60.

Looking at it another way, according to the info above, your average order amount would be $30. This comes by dividing the order sum by the number of orders ($150 ÷ 5 orders). However, to get an even more accurate picture, it's important to understand that the mean order amount is $10. The two higher orders skew your results. It may feel awesome to say your average order amount is $30, but if it's more likely your orders will be $10, then that's the number you should use when forecasting and coming up with your goal plans. If you DO sell the larger orders then you'll exceed your goals!

Forecasting

Forecasting is another term for projecting or guesstimating what you expect to achieve in the future. It is usually based on historical data, what your business has done in the past, and with an idea of how you plan to grow. Forecasting helps plan for marketing, increasing prospects into your funnel and improving conversion rates.

In business planning, customers ARE numbers and success IS a numbers game. The more people you talk to about your business and products, the more you will get to convert. The way to improve their conversion is to treat them like more than just a number, a friend, a person, a family, a dream.

Conversion Rate

Another way to improve your revenue is to improve your conversion rates in your funnels. In our candlemaker example from Step 7, if you can find ways to improve your checkout conversation rate to 30% (up from 20%) that will mean selling five candles per month instead of three. This will add an extra $20 in revenue without having to increase the number of prospects entering the funnel.

To improve your conversion rate at a specific step in your funnel, visit that area and ask yourself (or a customer, if they will share), "what is stopping my prospect from moving on to the next step?" Try and remove as many blocks as you can to improve your conversation rate. In a checkout process, that might mean having one checkout page instead of four individual steps or providing the convenience of a Paypal checkout. For a lead generation form, it could mean changing some of the required fields to optional. With regard to a website, it could be looking to optimize the placement, color or size of a button or rewriting the copy to be more compelling.

Web Analytics

Just like your general business numbers, it's a good idea to understand your Internet numbers. For websites, you should be tracking your web analytics and your social platform accounts should be providing you with reports that they call insights.

Web analytics track non-identifiable data from visitors to your site, including which pages they view, how long they stay on your site, how often they return, and how many pages they visit. If set up properly, they can even track if a visitor makes a purchase or completes another 'goal' like a lead form or email subscription, and generates funnel and conversion reports for you. (Google Analytics is a great, free resource, used by other apps like WordPress, Etsy and social sites.) There are plenty of how-to trainings online to educate yourself on the basics as well as the advanced features they offer.

Social platforms like Facebook, Instagram and even specialized sites like Etsy use **insights** which are based more on interaction and engagement than clicks or views. They usually include impressions, how many times a post or ad was displayed, and engagement which is how a visitor interacts with your content with a like, reaction, comment or share

Other marketplace platforms like Etsy, eBay and Zazzle, may have hybrid reporting which includes trackable info like page views and purchases as well as insights like hearts or comments.

After a month of business, review your analysts or insights. Where did you see good stats? What may have caused it? Can you learn from that situation and repeat it in the future? Where did something flop? How can you learn from it or tweak it to work better?

A/B Testing

If you are really into optimizing, you can look into your platform's capabilities for A/B testing. Most ad platforms, some email systems and even plugins for WordPress allow you to split your site visitors or email recipients into two groups, displaying content A to one group and different content B to the other group. A report is then generated to show which content converted better.

The trick is to just choose ONE aspect of the content to test, so you are only comparing one aspect at a time. For instance, test one ad with the same artwork and font styles but use different headline copy. Or, use the same font styles and headline copy but different artwork. If you change more than one aspect at a time, then you won't know what tweak really made the better impact to change your conversion rate.

You can use the A/B testing strategy in other areas of your business beyond website or ads. Make two versions of your product or have two different approaches when connecting with prospects. Try different things but remember to make single aspect tweaks—don't change everything! You are testing to see what works and what doesn't.

MOMPRENEUR STORIES

While every journey is unique, hearing stories of others already on the mompreneur path proves a very important truth—you aren't alone. We all took that scary and exciting first step. We have all failed at some point. Success, in whatever way you define it, is only attainable by learning from each failed step, taking a deep breath, picking up the next foot and taking the next step. Stumbles and falls are part of life. Getting up to try again or staying on the ground and giving up—those are choices. How do you choose to live?

THE MOMPRENEUR STORY OF

Jennifer Colucci

I was an entrepreneur long before I become a mother. For as long as I can remember, I've had the entrepreneur spark within me. I remember when I was six or seven making catalogs and selling them at a stand like other kids would sell lemonade. I took the large issue catalog from a department store, tore it apart and rebound it with construction paper into department sections. It was the first business idea that I came up with and executed, while my parents stood by supporting me. I did make a sale to a sweet lady who was driving by; she taught me that no matter your product or branding, it all really comes down to you. A motivated person with a bad product can still be a success. A perfect product without a driven person behind it can fall flat.

As I grew older, I participated in other entrepreneurial endeavors like selling handmade items at local boutiques, hunting for deals and reselling them for a profit, freelancing as a web designer and starting a few Internet marketing partnerships. Eventually, they fizzled out. It wasn't until I became bored with planning my wedding that I stumbled into building my first successful business: Creative Tradition. Out of the blue, my mother and I were invited to participate in a local handmade market. We had entered items into small fundraisers and holiday boutiques before, but this would be our first large market. As I was about to get married and planned to eventually have children, I saw this as an opportunity to get a jump start on my mompreneur business. I wanted to have a solid foundation built before I had my first child. I wanted to have all of the kinks worked out so that I wasn't building a business while learning to be a mom. I was already planning a business like a mompreneur before I actually became a mom.

I never expected it would take three years to officially become a mompreneur. I wasn't just working full time while building a business, I also changed jobs twice and experienced skin cancer followed by two miscarriages! Each day brought new challenges. They also brought new opportunities to grow and provided me with renewed belief in myself. Yes, some days were harder than others (and many ended in tears), but I lived through all of them to become the woman I am today. While I still get misty-eyed thinking about what I've lost, and what I've gained, I know that I would relive every single moment again to be who I am now. I am happy to be the mother to my precocious not-so-little little man, and I love being able to share my experiences and knowledge with you, in the hope that it propels you further along your own journey and without as many tears!

While building Creative Tradition for my own mompreneur motives, I was also intentionally setting it up to be a support for my mother. She had been a stay-at-home-mom for decades and I wanted something for her to invest her time, to help her understand her own worth and improve her self-confidence. As a partnership, it works out well for both of us. I love to design fabric and think up products, while my mother loves sewing and book keeping. In business terms, Creative Tradition is a hobby business. It provides an avenue to sell our creations and make a profit, but it isn't lucrative enough to support us both full-time.

The success of Creative Tradition led me to dream bigger; to imagine being a business owner and not just a hobbyist and to use my vast work experience to build a company that could grow with me, and be passed on to my son. Before jumping straight in like I did with Creative Tradition, I thought and planned out my vision for the new company, my career and family. If I wanted to be a millionaire, I needed a structure and foundation that supported those goals. That meant creating a corporation (with separate divisions for my different endeavors), processing payroll and being able to hire employees. I created Colucci Ventures with a vision and devised a plan to achieve it. It wasn't built on a whim or to get me through a gap on my resume. After playing at business-building and working in corporations and direct sales, I had uncovered one core truth about myself: I am an entrepreneur.

Up until that point, my career experience had been varied and diverse. I'd been part of marketing agencies, Internet service providers and web design firms. I'd worked in divisions including marketing, IT, ecommerce, business development and corporate strategy with titles like designer, developer, project manager, business analyst, manager and director. I'd been an independent consultant for direct sales companies and I'd worked in their corporate offices as well. Yet, each time I found myself hunting for my next position, I would question my career path. I felt as if I was playing hopscotch; jumping forward, to the side and then backwards. I loved what I did, but didn't see a clearly defined role that fit everything I could do. Most of the time that led to frustration as I tried to make positions grow to accommodate all I wanted to be. I would invest so much of my time, energy and care, knowing that I could help the company grow and yet without the authority to follow through, I felt as if I was just wasting my time. I worked well under leaders, but not being able to have a hand on the rudder always left me feeling powerless and ineffective.

One day, a week into a new job, I had an epiphany. I was six months post-partem with my son and I realized I was spending my life driving and working. I was leaving the house by 6 a.m. and getting home around 8 p.m. This left little to no time for my son. Our only interactions were getting ready in the morning, car rides on the way to day care or getting ready for bed. I wasn't happy. I was missing my son's milestones and was becoming depressed at the realization that he would most likely be my only child. Time was of the essence. I realized that this might be my only chance to experience motherhood and I was missing it for the sake of a job—and one I didn't even really care about.

So, I changed the direction of my life.

After years of building a career, I made a different choice. I chose to set aside 'Career Jenn' for 'Mom Jenn'. It was difficult releasing the major part of myself that had defined me for so many years. It was an adjustment, financially relying on one income. Yet, it was worth every tear and scrimped penny. I was able to focus on my most important job right then: being a mom. At the same time, I knew that there was more for me than solely being a mom. I loved raising my son, but I was still a woman with talent and ambition, so I started doing freelance web design to 'stay in the game'. During this time, something miraculous happened: I became happy! I was able to work with women, helping them build their brands and businesses; and still have time to take my son to playdates, parks and mommy-and-me classes. Not only was it the best of both mom and business worlds, but my decisions and actions had significant impact on the success of my business and my family. After a year of trying out my services as a sole proprietorship, I was ready to do it right and started my first corporation: Colucci Ventures.

I felt as if everything was in line with my life. And then, my husband was laid-off.

Although I was making an income, it was nowhere close enough to support our entire family's expenses. In a single moment, I went from a care-free momma 'playing' at business ownership, to a nose-to-the-grindstone momma on a mission to provide for her family. For three months I focused more on 'Entrepreneur Jenn' than 'Mom Jenn'. I didn't stop to think about it or feel fear for doing new things—I didn't have time. I set and hit amazing sales goals that I wouldn't have ever dreamed of before. I was so ecstatic for what I was accomplishing for us. With each day, I knew I could do it and understood that if I had the time and applied myself, my business and I would be a success.

But, I wasn't taking care of my son the way I wanted to (the reason I was a stay-at-home-mom in the first place). Plus, I wasn't able to interact with my husband aside from logistics. I was working ALL of the time. If I wasn't sleeping, I was working and when I was sleeping, I was worrying about clients I had to call, leads I needed to follow up with, what was next on my to do list, etc.

That's when I crashed…hard.

It took my husband going to the Emergency Room for me to realize how far I was pushing myself and how much it was impacting my family.

The day had started with us in Las Vegas with a flat tire and ended with us in Southern California in the ER, with my husband strapped to an EKG machine. We were in Las Vegas that weekend so that I could attend a direct sales convention. It had been a whirlwind with me visiting relatives in the gaps of free time I could find. Although my husband felt sick to his stomach the night before our trip to the ER, I still got up early the next day and set off to attend my next event. On the way to the convention center, a well-placed rock slashed one of my tires. As I waited for roadside assistance, I stared at a caution sign on the road. Fate, as it seems, was forcing me to take the time to analyze my recent choices.

The night before, I had decided to take on another business endeavor. I was excited and nervous about it, but I was determined—stubbornly so. Then the flat tire happened and the mocking caution sign was placed before me. I took them both as a divine sign of intervention. I needed to slow down and proceed with caution, right now. It was not the time to speed up and add more to my already full plate. It was time to slow down and be aware of my surroundings. So, instead of proceeding to the convention, I returned to my relative's home and really took notice of my husband's condition. While he didn't look terrible, I wanted to get him home, in his own bed where he could recuperate. I skipped my last event and we drove home to Southern California. My husband rested while I took care of our son. I got back to work and tried to get a handle on the emotional backlash of the morning's activities— decisions made, divine intervention and a long car ride home. I checked on my husband and he looked worse. He wasn't able to keep anything down and it was getting late. We had a choice to make—head to an urgent care center or go straight to the emergency room. As he was unemployed, we opted for the cheaper option. With a two-year-old in tow, we arrived at the urgent care just before closing. They checked his vitals and after seeing an abnormal EKG, they urged us to head to the emergency room.

There's nothing like a possible heart issue with the love of your life to make you forget about everything else.

As I drove to the emergency room, I mentally reprioritized my entire life.

"Family comes first," I'd always say, but now I really meant it. I didn't care how much it cost to bring my husband home alive and healthy. All the money in the world and successful business empires that I dreamt of building would amount to nothing without him.

Our local relatives met me at the hospital and took our son home with them so that I could focus all my attention on helping my husband. At one point, he had to be taken for further tests, so he gave me his wedding ring to hold. There I was, living my greatest fear, alone in an empty hospital room, wearing my husband's ring on my finger, unable to do anything to change my situation. For the first time in my life, I felt powerless. I was at the mercy of others, praying and willing my husband to return to me.

As it turns out, the issue wasn't his heart, but a severe case of dehydration. The experience, however; was the wake-up call our family needed. I took a photo of that empty hospital room because I knew it was a memory that would haunt and inspire me for the rest of my life. It was a glimpse into the future of what was at the end of the path we were on: over-hustling and setting ourselves last, if at all. It would be the end of the path, either for him, or for me, and the journey would not have been memorable or enjoyable at all. That's what stress can do to you.

It took us nearly two months to work through all the negativity that the stress had caused. We made changes; we refocused our priorities on family and our own self-care, and then created a new vision for our future. A successful life was no longer about our bank account, job title or the size of our house. A healthy, joyful, loving family who followed their passions free of financial stress was our new definition for a well-lived life.

Through it all, I am grateful that I have been able to experience motherhood as a working mom, a stay-at-home-mom, a work-from-home-mom and a business-owning-mom. I've felt the dependency of relying completely on my husband's income and I've felt the guilt of leaving my child in daycare all day. I've felt the stress of being the sole breadwinner (while potty training a toddler, too.) I've learned that life on the other side isn't always better—it's just different. You have to choose which 'different' is right for you and your family.

Success is about finding the balance
of what you want out of life and
what you are willing to give to make it happen.

Making a choice doesn't mean it's your forever choice. It's about making the choice that is right for you and your family at that time, and then living with it until it no longer fits.

After such a journey, working with mompreneurs is my ultimate dream job. It's not just about building businesses, it's about building a legacy for other families. I'm not just helping moms succeed. I am helping moms put their little girls through ballet or fund their family's first-ever college graduates. Even more important, I am helping moms show their kids that they are so much more than one-sided caregivers. Moms are dreamers, builders and business owners. They are driven, confident and successful. Moms can be, do and have anything they set they set their mind to achieving.

I have a dream—a mental image I revisit often when I meditate or need a dose of motivation. It came to my mind vividly, when I experienced Way To Shine's "Awaken to Your Purpose" guided imagery for the first time. I'm on a stage, looking out upon the faces of thousands of smiling, joyful women. I am the spotlight—my inspirational energy flows through me and onto all of these women. My light illuminates their faces just as my words have inspired and impacted their lives. That vision is what keeps me shining. I know there are women I have yet to meet who may depend on me. I may not directly touch their lives, yet I know in my soul that I will leave an impression on them.

That vision is the spark that has ignited my soul.

I now have a blazing fire within me that keeps me going throughout the day. When I am feeling tired or frustrated, I look to that fire to keep me energized and moving towards my goal. That fire is You. I know there are other moms out there, just like me, just like you, who are craving support and depending on me to share the experiences I've had and the knowledge I've learned throughout my own journey.

That's why I wrote this book.

For YOU. Because you have it in you to be so much more. You can be a dreamer, a builder, a business owner. You can be driven, confident and successful. You just have to make the choice and take your first step.

You can connect with Jenn at www.JenniferColucci.com
or the Successful Mompreneurs group on Facebook.

THE MOMPRENEUR STORY OF

Martie Wynn

I was an entrepreneur long before I was a mother. As a child, I watched my parents become entrepreneurs. They owned a restaurant before starting a family and at one point we even had a horse-cookie making business. They were always searching for alternative avenues to stay out of the standard, corporate nine-to-five job.

My father would always say, "Just let me try. Don't limit me to what I can do." I grew up optimistic about the opportunities I could create for myself. My parents showed me that I could do anything I wanted to do. I had to work hard to get it, but when I did the work, the benefits would come. I live that philosophy; at 14, I got a work permit and worked at a deli for the summer. I've worked ever since.

My first taste of being an entrepreneur was in middle school when I took a home economics class. I designed and created a few fashionable shirts and then sold them at a boutique. Interestingly, 10 years later I saw the exact same style shirt for sale in a store.

After graduating high school and then working fulltime while going to college, I knew that I was never going to be satisfied with the corporate world and a typical nine-to-five job. Back then I did it, because that's what you did, but it never felt like the right direction for me. I enjoyed investing my time to improve the company, but I never really felt that I was contributing in a bigger way. Sure, I got a paycheck which supported me, but I felt that I wasn't making the impact that I could.

I was in the corporate world for 10 years before I decided to leave and become a real estate agent. As an agent with a well-known brokerage you are supported with branding, training and other resources, but you are still an entrepreneur. You don't sell houses unless you put in the work. I knew I could maximize my time and augment my commissions by bringing in additional revenue by providing services to other real estate professionals and investors. I started a transaction coordination company, working for myself from home and supporting three brokers and 10 agents. I did that for a year and a half, until I moved back to the Bay Area and partnered with investors to create a real estate investment company, purchasing distressed homes, renovating them and reselling them again.

Life was wonderful. The company was doing well; we were flipping 10-12 properties a month and my husband and I were happy. Then, we got the wonderful news that we were expecting. Everyone was so excited for us! But, after I had my first child, I suddenly felt like I had fallen off the face of the Earth!

My company may have thought that after becoming a mother I wouldn't want to work, but for my sanity I needed to keep going. I needed to keep setting goals, creating both financial freedom and time freedom for my family. So I decided to continue my real estate business and started doing extra broker price opinions on the side. I began to research other side businesses, specifically network marketing companies with strong ecommerce options and joined two diverse companies with products and compensation plans I love. Together, they have allowed me to stay at home to raise my children and continue in a reduced capacity as a real estate agent. I look forward to the time my daughter and son will be ready for school so that I can invest more time in my businesses. Right now though, I'm choosing to stay home with my kids, which means I am not putting in the time that the businesses deserve, and I'm okay with that.

Throughout this journey, I've learned a lot about myself. I never thought I would be a stay-at-home mom, building three businesses that allow me to raise my kids. For me, the most important thing is balance. Finding balance between mother, wife and entrepreneur in a way that you don't lose yourself. I know I'm a different person now because I am a mother; it's a personal journey that is making me a better person. Life changed when I became a mom, and it all worked out the way it was supposed to. Even though I felt disgruntled when my company thought I wasn't going to return to work, I now know that was an experience that needed to occur in order for me to become the mompreneur I am today. Prior to becoming a mother, I was more entrepreneurial in my thoughts than in my actions. After having children, my 'Why' got bigger, so I started taking action, things went into motion and came into fruition.

If I could go back and do things differently, I would have become an entrepreneur earlier. It took me nine months after having my first child before I became motivated about doing something besides real estate. I wish I could have started earlier: investing in my personal growth, health and in learning better ways to manage my time and business. It would have been a lot easier to add an extra business into an existing schedule. If I had known then, what I know now, life would be a whole lot easier and much less stressful. And yet, those experiences are what has brought me here today.

Some days I feel like I am taking on a lot in my business as well as my personal development, but success to me is all about the small wins. It's not about the big moments. It takes many small blocks of success to build that big achievement. To build a business, or raise a child, you have to take many steps. With each step, with each thing you do, no matter how small it is, you move yourself, your business or your child forward. If you do that, then you've succeeded for the day. Although I don't feel that my businesses are as successful as I want them to be right now, I see the potential my businesses have and where they can go.

Success doesn't always have a monetary value and each mompreneur should know what drives them in their business. With my latest real estate transaction, I was most excited by helping first-time buyers experience the joy of their first home. The gratitude and emotions I witnessed influenced me more than my well-earned commission.

My vision is to build a community with my businesses. I want to build teams and supportive networks of real estate agents, consultants and leaders who are working toward creating their own outcomes and spreading the word to help others do the same.

I know my vision is grand and the biggest obstacle I have to overcome is creating time. Finding the time, making the time and scheduling the time is my biggest challenge. Working from home, with two children at different stages, means inconsistent schedules. (Getting one down for a nap while the other battles with you until she finally falls asleep on your lap, moments before her brother wakes up, leaves little room for business activities!) As a mompreneur, I have to choose where to spend my time. Do I sacrifice sleep? Quality time with my children? Family time? Making dinner? Cleaning? Which one do I skip? I can't do it all, but I can choose what to do now and what can wait for later. Sometimes, it's the dishes. Sometimes, it's the business. Right now, with two kids under four, I choose my kids. After all, as Jenn Colucci wrote, "it's the Mom that comes first in Mompreneur."

I want a lot for my children and my family. I want to be able to provide flexibility, opportunity and financial freedom for them. To me, financial freedom means not having to worry about where I can send my kids to school; not worrying about what happens if my car breaks down; not worrying about financing family vacations, or having enough time to go and do everything we want. I want to create residual income so my husband and I can be present for our kids. And, most importantly, I want be able to create the opportunity for my kids to decide whatever they want to pursue in sports, travel, hobbies and education. You never know what they will want or who they will become, and I want to have the money to keep them engaged in their passions.

Just like my parents did with me, I want to pass on my entrepreneurial spirit to my children. I want them to know they have the ability to do it, try it, and if it doesn't work, that's okay. I want them to know that they are individual and whatever makes them successful comes from within. It's what makes each person unique. There isn't just one way to live life or to become successful. I want them to be able to do whatever they want to do, whatever makes them happy.

I stay sane by imagining the future I am creating for my family. By staying home, building my businesses and raising my children, I know that I have committed myself to large goals. However; seeing how achieving those goals affects my family makes me so grateful to have made the choices I have.

I try to be in the moment. Running around trying to do everything, to be everything for everyone is unproductive and unsustainable. You will burn yourself out. Focus on being in the moment by managing your time, using a schedule and blocking out specific time for specific events. If I know my schedule for the day and have a (manageable) to-do list, most of the time it all gets done. I find myself feeling better about being with my kids and not taking calls, if I am in the moment with them when I need to be. In return, this helps me feel less guilty when I am on a call, watching them playing together, knowing that I have other quality time scheduled with them.

Don't be afraid to be selfish with your business. Sometimes we hire a babysitter and skip out on our date; sometimes my husband does his own thing and I leave the house to spend quality time with my business. The fear of missing out drives me to keep going and pushes me to work hard, so I can provide for my family in the way that I want. Although I still feel like I am at the beginning, when I look up to other mompreneurs, leaders and speakers and see that they are doing it—building empires and having more kids, I know it's doable! If they can do it, so can I. And, so can YOU!

Do it. Don't wait. If you think you don't have what it takes, think again. My father always told me, "Where there is a will, there is a way." There is so much support out there for you, so many tools, resources and groups to help you get started and keep going. Websites, ecommerce and social media have opened a whole new world of opportunities for moms like you and me who want to be entrepreneurs while raising our families. It took me a while to find a group of other like-minded mompreneurs, but when I did, I didn't feel alone anymore. This is such a journey and personal transformation that it gets to the point where it's not even about building a business anymore! It becomes all about life; about bettering yourself and your family. Everything else follows.

I end with one of my favorite quotes from author Courtney C. Stevens, "if nothing changes, nothing changes." If you want to change your family's situation, you need to make changes and take action toward your vision.

You can connect with Martie at www.MartieWynn.com.

THE MOMPRENEUR STORY OF

Shankari Paradee

My entrepreneurial journey started from the time I could pick up needle and thread. My mother has said that sewing is in my blood. She was a seamstress at a large suit company and my father created his own award-winning, vintage automobile upholstery business. I've dabbled in creating and selling jewelry and paintings and I've participated in several different network marketing companies. While being an entrepreneur has also been in the back of my mind, it wasn't until Sewl Sister that I felt I was really ready to embrace it. Besides, the fifth time's the charm, right?

My business, Sewl Sister, began shortly after I started designing my signature product, a Tea Tote to organize and carry your tea bags safely in your purse. I spent months designing, drawing and creating paper prototypes while my children colored next to me. I've always been a creator, turning nothing into something. I've also been naturally inquisitive, figuring out how things were made, taking the time to learn how I could make them myself. As I spent more time refining the pattern, I began to realize I wanted my business to be more than just a way to sell my designs, I wanted to be able to give back—in a huge way. Sewing feeds my soul and I know it has the power to do the same for others. I'm passionate about sharing sewing with a new generation of women. It's my vision to empower young women to learn how to sew and therefore provide for their family. It could be something as simple as learning how to hem pants or replace a button, or maybe even taking their newfound skills and starting their own business with it.

I also want to pass on sewing and entrepreneurism to my kids. I want them to know whatever they set their mind to, they can achieve. I want them to know it is okay to fail, so long as they fail forward. I've made so many mistakes in my jobs, businesses and my creations. The trick is not to give up if something doesn't work and most importantly, never give up on yourself!

I've found that believing in yourself and working past your own personal fear is the hardest part of being a mompreneur. I feel as if my Tea Tote is my baby and I want everyone to love it just as much as I do, its mom. When I first started sharing it with everyone, I was afraid of what they would think of me and my product. It has taken me time, and help from my coach, to work through the fear and personal judgements toward myself.

Fear is going to show up, no matter what you do. So don't be afraid to start. Take that first step and just START. The first step doesn't need to be a huge step; it could just be talking to someone about your idea. You never know, they could become your future business or support partner. Then, once you start, don't be afraid to fail. It's okay to stumble, to fall, to fail, but fail forward. Get up and take another step forward. Take steps slowly, even if it seems hard and keep going forward.

The biggest impact I've had in my business so far, is connecting with like-minded people and asking them for support. Finding the right mentors and guidance is key—it has propelled me so much further than trying to figure it all out by myself.

I know I'm a success right now, as a mom. I recently figured out who I was and how my success as a mom is because of my kids. Knowing they are a success is my success. I didn't strive to become successful, I realized it had already started and all I had to do was step into and own it. Success as an entrepreneur is a bit trickier. It is the biggest compliment I can get as a mom when people tell me how my kids are well-behaved, well-mannered and well-spoken. It means the world to me, knowing we are doing a good job as parents. As an entrepreneur, I feel like I'm still chasing success. For me, success is being able to spend time with my family without the pressure of worrying about how much it will cost or how long it will take. I want to leverage time and money to work for me and my family so we can enjoy time together.

As mompreneurs, we are all legacy moms; our goal is for the betterment of not just our own lives, but the lives of our children, and their children too. When we light the torch to inspire ourselves, our children carry it on and become a beacon to others. The legacy we leave isn't just our success but also our failures. When I fail and my children see it, I fail forward because they are there to support me. They give me a hug and say, "It's okay, Mommy. You will try again." That's what the Legacy Mom Movement is all about. It's a supportive Facebook group I founded for moms to share and support each other in both success, failure and everything in between.

So when I fail, I give myself grace, and so should you. Each step I take, no matter how slowly it takes, is one step closer to reaching my vision for the future of my business and my family. I am okay working it part-time, splitting time between my family and my dreams. Besides, doing it part-time is better than doing it no-time!

You can connect with Shankari at www.SewlSister.com
or the Legacy Mom Movement group on Facebook.

BUSINESS IDEAS

You may have been daydreaming, sketching or playing around with your business idea for a while now. Or, you may have the entrepreneurial spark fluttering around your soul trying to find that one, significant idea to set ablaze. In case of the latter, here are some ideas for businesses, services or products to help ignite your spark.

Set out a piece of paper and get ready to write down any notes as you read through this list. These suggestions may spark the perfect idea for you, and you want to be ready for inspiration!

Start by making a list of anything that other people have said you are good at. If you can't recall, ask your close friends what they think are your strengths—what you're good at doing or making. Think of it another way: what does your family always ask you to help with? Can you think back to a moment when you saw someone else's product and thought, "I could do that better!"

Find your passion and understand your competencies; then think of ways to make money from them!

Feel free to jot down your own ideas or visit SuccessfulMompreneur.com for more inspiration.

ART & DESIGN BUSINESS IDEAS

If you find your bliss while creating art, try some of these business ideas:

- Start a print-on-demand shop at Zazzle, CafePress or Studio66 to sell your artwork on anything and everything from canvas, mugs to blankets to shower curtains.
- Sell post cards, prints and originals at craft shows or local gift shops.
- Provide graphic design services including logo design, layout or web design.
- Create lasting memories by becoming a wedding, event, portrait, family, maternity or newborn photographer.
- Sell images, including vector graphics and photography at stock image sites like iStock or CreativeMarket.
- Sell your artwork or designs as fabric, wrapping paper or wallpaper at Spoonflower.
- Offer consignment work such as painting pet portraitures, corporate sculptures or murals.
- Team up with an author and become a children's book illustrator or, write your own story to go along with your art.
- Teach classes at art supply stores, birthday parties or mom's night out events.
- Join a network marketing company like Send Out Cards.

ANIMAL-FOCUSED BUSINESS IDEAS

If you love all animals, or a specific breed in particular, try some of these business ideas:

- Start a pet shop, shelter or zoo.
- Sell treats, costumes or toys online or at local markets.
- Create a monthly box subscription service with toys, snacks and product samples.
- Become a dog sitter, walker or trainer.
- Design, build and decorate cat climbers, dog houses or other unique enclosures.
- Write a blog or book about pet care training, DIY hacks or even a treat cookbook.
- Teach children appreciation for animals with a mobile petting zoo, horse riding lessons or rent-a-pet service.
- Join a network marketing company like pawTree or Yuppy Puppy City Kitty.

BEAUTY & FASHION BUSINESS IDEAS

If you are passionate about looking your best, try some of these business ideas:

- Start a beauty salon, clothing boutique or accessory shop.
- Create a clothing line.
- Offer your services as a mobile spray tanner.
- Create your own lip glosses, soaps or bath salts.
- Become a stylist, beautician or personal shopper.
- Connect with modeling agencies or photographers to be an on-site stylist.
- Teach others how to create their own beauty products, apply make-up or style hair with online videos or at in-home parties.
- Join a network marketing company like Arbonne, Avon, Beauty Counter, Jamberry, LulaRoe, Mary Kay or Thirty-One.

KID-CENTRIC BUSINESS IDEAS

If you are inspired to interact, educate or entertain children, try some of these business ideas:

- Start an infant, preschool or afterschool day care center.
- Sell hand-crafted toys.
- Open a second-hand consignment store or pop-up shop.
- Create a monthly box subscription service with age-specific toys, apparel, personal care, art supplies or science experiments.
- Offer your services as a nanny, sleep trainer or tutor.
- Write a book about your journey as a mother and your experiences with multiples, rainbow babies, or a child with special needs.
- Teach teens life skills like how to manage money or interview for a job.
- Join a network marketing company like Barefoot Books, Usborne Books & More or Simply Fun.

CRAFTS & DIY BUSINESS IDEAS

If you love to create, craft, or do-it-yourself try some of these business ideas:

- Start a DIY blog that chronicles your projects, provides video tutorials and reviews tools and products.
- Sew quilts, baby gift sets, stuffed animals, costumes, or home décor.
- Design accessories like jewelry, hair bows or bow ties.
- Knit or crochet scarves, hats, or toys.
- Create kits or tutorials for others to follow your patterns and instructions to do their own DIY of your creations.
- Recycle or upcycle furniture.
- Write a how-to or pattern book.
- Teach sewing, knitting, scrapbooking, or soap-making as private lessons or group classes.
- Join a network marketing company like Creative Memories, Origami Owls or Stampin' Up.

FOOD LOVERS BUSINESS IDEAS

If you enjoy cooking, baking, decorating or feeding people, try some of these business ideas:

- Start an eatery location, foot truck or cart.
- Sell baked goods, canned goods or even pet treats at farmer's markets or Etsy.
- Create a food or meal delivery service.
- Become a caterer or special occasion chef.
- Write a cookbook or create a recipe blog.
- Teach in-home cooking lessons or create videos of you demonstrating how to cook.
- Join a network marketing company like Pampered Chef, Tara at Home or WildTree.

FITNESS & HEALTH BUSINESS IDEAS

If you are passionate about nutrition or exercise, try some of these business ideas:

- Start a gym, yoga or barre studio.
- Sell weekly fitness seminars to corporations to provide educational lunch-and-learns or even lead sample exercise routines to their employees.
- Create a monthly box subscription service with healthy snacks, supplements, fitness gear or apparel.
- Become a certified nutritionist, personal trainer, yoga or Zumba instructor.
- Write a weight-loss, health or fitness book.
- Teach specialized sports activities by becoming a pitching or hitting coach, golf or tennis instructor.
- Lead boot camps at local parks or join a franchise like Fit4Mom.
- Join a network marketing company like BeachBody, Herbalife or IsaGenix.

HOME-FOCUSED BUSINESS IDEAS

If you find joy in cleaning or decorating, try some of these business ideas:

- Start a housecleaning, pool, painting or handy-mom service.
- Become an interior designer or stage homes for open houses.
- Visit homes and help people declutter and organize.
- Rent additional space for parties or as offices or even lease properties.
- Provide offices with plant-watering or holiday decorating services.
- Decorate homes or offices for each season or holiday.
- Become a real estate agent, broker or transaction coordinator.
- Join a network marketing company like Aerus, Gold Canyon, Scentsy or Simply Said.

MUSIC BUSINESS IDEAS

If singing or playing music lights you up, try some of these business ideas:

- Start an after-school music program for kids.
- Sell your songs and albums on Bandzoogle.
- Become a DJ for parties, events or clubs.
- Create an eCourse teaching people how to learn the guitar or piano.
- Write songs for other performers.
- Perform live at local venues or events.
- Become a private instructor, singing coach or manager.

PARTY-PLANNING BUSINESS IDEAS

If you like to throw a pin-worthy party, try some of these business ideas:

- Start a wedding, event or party planning business.
- Design digital party printables like invitations, goodie bags and other decorations.
- Rent event supplies like tables, chairs, linens and reusable decorations.
- Sell handmade party decorations or favors on Etsy.
- Design wedding invitations.
- Write a party-theme ideas book or how to plan your wedding workbook.
- Become a party entertainer such as a clown, magician, princess or super hero.
- Join a network marketing company like Tastefully Simple or Traveling Vineyard.

PLANT & GARDENING BUSINESS IDEAS

If you have a green thumb or a special "sixth sense" when it comes to floral arrangements, try some of these business ideas:

- Start a gardening or landscape design firm.
- Sell your organic herbs, succulents or potted plants at farmer markets.
- Create plant-your-own aquaponics, terrariums, or fairy garden kits to sell on Etsy.
- Write a blog about your growing journey and tips.
- Teach planting or pruning classes, local garden centers or expos.

SERVICE-BASED BUSINESS IDEAS

If you have specific training, certifications or professional experience, try some of these business ideas:

- Start a financial planning or accounting firm.
- Open your own therapy or counseling practice.
- Become a life coach or motivational speaker.
- Offer your services as a virtual assistant or personal assistant.
- Deliver groceries, meals or provide other concierge services like dry-cleaning pick-up.
- Join Uber, Lyft or better yet, HopSkipDrive or Safr.
- Bring job seekers and hiring companies together as a recruiter, resume writer or HR consultant.
- Develop web sites or apps, provide tech support or become a business consultant.
- Sell insurance or process medical billing.
- Become a tutor or academic assistance provider.

RESELLER BUSINESS IDEAS

If you get a thrill when you find a great deal, try some of these business ideas:

- Open an antiques or collectibles shop.
- Collect and resell collectibles you are passionate about — everything from toys, books, art and memorabilia.
- Organize, advertise and run garage or estate sales.
- Start a consignment store, selling other's items in-store or online.

WELLNESS BUSINESS IDEAS

If you are into holistic remedies or flow of energies, try some of these business ideas:

- Open a massage, zen yoga studio or wellness center.
- Sell your handmade soaps, lotions, oils or candles on Etsy.
- Create chakra stone or crystal gift sets with informational booklets.
- Record your own meditations and sell them on Bandzoogle.
- Conduct group meditations at businesses, hotels or parks.
- Become a reiki practitioner.
- Join a network marketing company like DoTerra or Young Living.

WORD & LANGUAGE BUSINESS IDEAS

If you have a way with words or turns of phrase, try some of these business ideas:

- Start a weekly blog to grow your following and earn money from advertisers.
- Become a language translator.
- Write children's books.
- Write a book (or several!) and self-publish them with CreateSpace.
- Teach writing workshops in-person or online.
- Provide your copywriting, editing, or beta reading skills to companies or other writers.

MOMPRENEURS, INSPIRATION & RESOURCES

Visit SuccessfulMompreneur.com to be inspired by more mompreneur stories and business ideas. You'll also find access to more resources including workbooks, exercise templates and other goodies to support you on your journey as a successful mompreneur.

Connect with other mompreneurs at the Successful Mompreneurs Facebook group.

ABOUT THE AUTHOR

Jennifer Colucci is an author, artist and mompreneur. Her books cover her experiences in business, technology, personal empowerment and motherhood.

She has helped more than one hundred businesses grow in industries including beauty, wellness, transportation, technology, food, real estate, retail, professional services, hospitality, network marketing, finance, start-ups, communities and personalities.

She lives in Southern California, with her husband and son.

www.ingramcontent.com/pod-product-compliance
Lightning Source LLC
Chambersburg PA
CBHW071553200326
41519CB00021BB/6730